A CENTURY DOWNTOWN

A VISUAL HISTORY OF LOWER MANHATTAN · BY MATT KAPP

powerHouse Books

Brooklyn, New York

"CHANGE IS THE
ONLY CONSTANT."

—HERACLITUS

FOREWORD

I'VE BEEN IN THE REAL-ESTATE
BUSINESS FOR OVER 60 YEARS, so I've
been through a few up-and-down cycles:
the 1950s, the oil crisis and stagflation of
the 1970s, and the recession of the early
1990s. More recently, of course, we've
been through the dot-com collapse, the
9/11 attacks, the Great Recession following
the collapse of Lehman Brothers, and
superstorm Sandy. From these experiences,
I've learned first and foremost that you
should never bet against New York. *Never*.
This town always comes back—stronger
than ever.

After 9/11, there was a great debate over
what should be built at the World Trade
Center site. It was quintessential New
York: passionate, loud and fractious. But
one thing was clear—the new World

Trade Center needed to be much more than
what it had been before. Of course, we all
agreed that our primary responsibility was
to commemorate those we lost. At the same
time, however, we had to restore the
commerce that has defined the lower tip of
Manhattan throughout the city's history.

When I started rebuilding the World
Trade Center, everyone told me I was
crazy. All I heard was "You'll never get
it finished," "You'll never get it financed,"
"Nobody is going to want to work in
a World Trade Center tower again,"
"Downtown is finished as a business
district." Sometimes great things take
a long time to do. Rebuilding the World
Trade Center has taken 18 years so far,
and it will probably be another 5 years
before we are finished.

One reason that the project has taken so long
is because it is a public-private partnership,
and the public side keeps changing. We are
building on a site in New York City that is
owned by the Port Authority and overseen
by the governors of New York and New
Jersey, and over the past 18 years there
have been four governors of New York, six
governors of New Jersey, and three mayors
of New York City! And every time one of
them came into office, each with their own
agenda, they said, "Stop! Wait! I need to
approve this." There are always going to be
people and factors outside of your control,
but you can't lose focus.

My company opened 7 World Trade Center
five years after 9/11. Designed by my good
friend David Childs, of Skidmore, Owings
& Merrill, it was the first "green" office

tower in New York City history. It is one of the safest buildings ever built, and a model not just for all the other World Trade Center buildings but also for the modern American skyscraper. In 2013, we opened 4 World Trade Center, the first new building on the original 16-acre site. With it, we re-introduced a 200-foot stretch of Greenwich Street that hadn't existed since the 1960s. And in 2018, we opened 3 World Trade Center, whose floors are column-free to create an open workspace environment—key for cutting-edge companies in brainpower-driven businesses.

The new downtown isn't your grandfather's Wall Street. While we were rebuilding the World Trade Center, Lower Manhattan emerged as a new model of what is best and most dynamic about New York. The residential population has tripled, and the neighborhood is now one of the city's most desirable places to live and raise a family. Nearly everyone who works here either walks or takes mass transit to work—downtown has the highest live/work ratio in the U.S. That also makes it one of the greenest neighborhoods in the country. It's also still the international capital of finance and has remade itself into the new media-and-entertainment capital of America. The area south of Chambers Street now boasts more than 800 technology, advertising, media, and information companies, ranging from ambitious tech start-ups to legacy media companies like Condé Nast and HarperCollins.

Two years ago, we opened our new Four Seasons hotel, just a block from the World Trade Center, along with Wolfgang Puck's first restaurant in New York. The private residences upstairs at 30 Park Place sold exceptionally well. And my wife, Klara, and I moved in last year, so I now have a one-block commute to the office!

I invite you to visit the new downtown and see for yourself all the great things that are happening here. In the meantime, I encourage you to read this book. It will take you on a remarkable visual journey, guided by a fascinating historical narrative that sheds new light on the extraordinary resurgence of Lower Manhattan.

See you around the neighborhood!

LARRY A. SILVERSTEIN

TABLE OF CONTENTS

1919–1974

1976–2019

"I NEVER MADE A SPEECH BEFORE IN MY LIFE," Charlie Chaplin bellowed into a megaphone above a sea of bobbing fedoras, bowlers, and newsboy caps just after noon on the second Monday of April 1918. "But I believe I can make one now!" Chaplin was at the peak of his fame and the highest-paid movie star in the world. Office workers out on their lunch break began to gather at the steps of the U.S. Sub-Treasury Building at 26 Wall Street to see what all the commotion was about. Within half an hour, the crowd had swollen as far as Broadway to the west and William Street to the east.

THE RISE OF WALL STREET

F

FLANKING CHAPLIN WAS HIS PAL, "KING OF HOLLYWOOD" Douglas Fairbanks, with whom he would soon co-found the United Artists movie studio. "Money is needed to support the great army and navy of Uncle Sam," Chaplin impressed upon the crowd. "This very minute the Germans occupy a position of advantage, and we have got to get the dollars ... so that we can drive that old devil, the kaiser, out of France!"

YOU
BUY a
LIBERTY BOND
LEST I PERISH

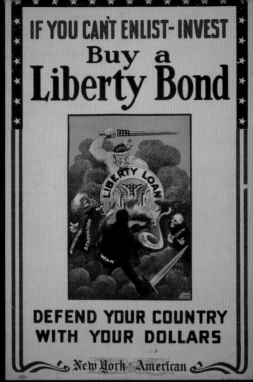

IF YOU CAN'T ENLIST-INVEST
Buy a
Liberty Bond

LIBERTY LOAN

DEFEND YOUR COUNTRY
WITH YOUR DOLLARS

New York American

THAT LIBERTY SHALL NOT
PERISH FROM THE EARTH
BUY LIBERTY BONDS
FOURTH LIBERTY LOAN

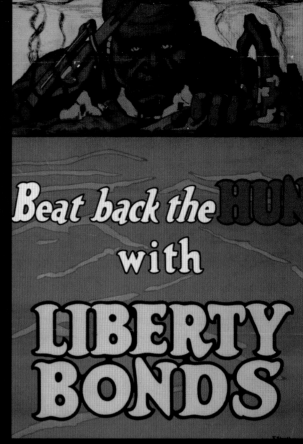

Beat back the HUN
with
LIBERTY
BONDS

MU
CHILDREN
AND M
PLEAD

BO

Bring in your '50 and take
home YOUR BOND!

THIRD
ISSUE
LIBERTY
BONDS

CIGARS

nited Cigar Stores Company

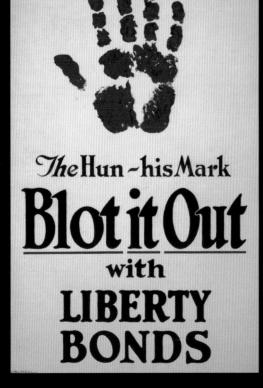

The Hun ~ his Mark
Blot it Out
with
LIBERTY
BONDS

Sunrise or Sunset
Own a
Liberty Bond
A Liberty Bond is a US Government
Bond The best security in the World
It bears interest and is readily saleable

"Shall we be more
tender with our
dollars than with
the Lives of our sons"
W.G. McAdoo
Secretary of the Treasury
Buy a United States Government Bond of the

Lib
P

Mile after mile
of desolation a
toll.

Liber
Buy

HELLO!
THIS IS LIBERTY SPEAKING

keep
these
off
the U.S.A

THE TREASURY ENLISTED CHAPLIN AND FAIRBANKS AS LEADING PITCHMEN FOR THE BIGGEST MARKETING BLITZ THE COUNTRY HAD EVER SEEN.

The U.S. had been at war with Germany for a year, and thousands of American servicemen were pouring into France daily to reinforce Allied positions on the Western Front. The war was swiftly draining the nation's finances, so the Treasury turned to the public to help underwrite the effort, in the form of tax-exempt "Liberty" bonds, and enlisted Chaplin and Fairbanks as leading

The Armistice Day parade, November 11, 1918, marking the end of hostilities between the Allies and Germany.

pitchmen for the biggest marketing blitz the country had ever seen. Fairbanks assumed the bullhorn from Chaplin. "Hello, everybody! I used to work down here about 10 years ago. Are you folks good Americans? Have you bought Liberty bonds?" he cajoled the crowd.

The duo's patriotic pep rally drew more than 20,000 spectators, the *New-York Tribune* reported the next morning, making it "the largest crowd in the history of the financial lane." Chaplin and Fairbanks spent the next month crisscrossing the country hawking the bonds, which would ultimately raise $20 billion for the war ($343 billion in 2019 dollars) and return up to 4.75 percent to bondholders. Liberty bonds would be reissued by the federal government 84 years later to help finance the rebuilding of Lower Manhattan after 9/11.

The Treaty of Versailles formally ended the war in June 1919. It was a major turning point for the country—and for Wall Street. The "Great War" had converted America from debtor to creditor nation for the first time, paving the way for Lower Manhattan to assume the mantle of financial capital of the world from London's Square Mile.

THE WAR PAVED THE WAY FOR LOWER MANHATTAN TO ASSUME THE MANTLE OF FINANCIAL CAPITAL OF THE WORLD.

19
20

19 20

1920–1924

JUST BEFORE NOON ON SEPTEMBER 16, 1920, a horse-drawn cart, with a canvas tarp draped over its cargo, rattled up Wall Street past the grand colonnade of the National City Bank Building and rolled to a stop across from the marble-clad, fortress-like House of Morgan, at 23 Wall Street, beneath the spot where Charlie Chaplin and Douglas Fairbanks had given their Liberty-bonds pep rally two years before. The driver cast off the horse's reins, stepped down from the carriage, and vanished into the lunchtime crowd. Moments later, with the last toll of Trinity Church's noon bells still hanging in the air, the cart exploded in a fireball that billowed 20 stories skyward. Thirty people were killed instantly, scores more grievously injured. Among the dead were brokers, clerks, secretaries, telegraphers, stenographers, and messengers. It was the worst terrorist attack the country had ever seen.

BLOODY THURSDAY

Thirty people were killed instantly by the explosion.

A GHOSTLY SILENCE FOLLOWED THE BLAST, save for the patter of broken glass hitting the pavement. "Almost in front of the steps leading up to the Morgan bank was the mutilated body of a man," observed Associated Press reporter George Weston, who'd been in the lobby of a nearby building when the blast went off. "Other bodies, most of them silent in death, lay nearby. As I gazed horror-stricken at the sight, one of these forms, half naked, and seared with burns, started to rise. It struggled, then toppled and fell lifeless into the gutter." All that was left of the wagon "were the axles, a few shattered spokes and a small heap of tangled metal," *The New York Times* reported. The horse's front hooves landed in front of Trinity Church, two blocks away.

Such was the force of the explosion that "a man walking along John Street, five blocks north, was felled by a four-inch length of pipe crashing on the base of his neck," wrote Edward Robb Ellis in his sprawling history, *The Epic of New York City*. All they ever found of Edward Sweet, the millionaire proprietor of Sweet's seafood restaurant, was his ring finger, ring still attached. "As you walked down the street," wrote a *Daily News* reporter, "you smelled a particular odor that soldiers came to know in France. It made your stomach convulse."

Within minutes, the bell rang on the floor the New York Stock Exchange, halting trading. Telephone switchboards south of 42nd Street jammed as hundreds of police officers, firefighters, medics, Red Cross nurses, and troops from the 22nd Infantry arrived on the scene, attending to the dying and removing the dead. Ordinary citizens rose to remarkable acts of heroism, too. Immediately after the blast, instead of running to safer ground, 17-year-old Robinson & Co. office boy James Saul picked himself up, commandeered a nearby automobile, and began taxiing the injured to nearby Broad Street Hospital.

Boy Seizes Auto and Takes 30 Injured to the Hospital

Among the notable instances of rescue work following the explosion was that of James Saul, a red-headed, seventeen-year-old office boy, employed by Robinson & Co., 26 Exchange Place.

Knocked over and cut by the force of the explosion as he was running through the street in front of the Morgan Building, he picked himself up and began to load injured into a nearby automobile which he commandeered. He made four trips to Broad Street Hospital, carrying more than thirty persons.

Upon his return he could not find the owner of the automobile and, fearing the latter might be among the injured, turned the car over to the police at the Old Slip station. He lives at 2,868 Riggs Avenue, Brooklyn.

All that was left of the wagon was a "small heap of tangled metal," *The New York Times* reported.

Throngs of onlookers tried to get a glimpse of the carnage.

Around 3:30 that afternoon, as the dead were still being carried away, the Stock Exchange board of governors voted to reopen for business the next day. Cleanup crews worked all night to erase any trace of the carnage, likely sweeping away evidence that might have helped investigators identify the culprits. "Like a strong man who sticks to the line after binding up his wounds," *The Sun* reported, "Wall Street, from its lowly office boy to its most stately financier, went to work [the next day] with head up and teeth set, determined to show the world that business will proceed as usual despite bombs." A previously scheduled Constitution Day event in front of the Sub-Treasury Building turned into a mass rally in defiance of the attack, thousands of New Yorkers joining in renditions of "America the Beautiful" and "The Star-Spangled Banner." Otherwise it was business as usual, and by the end of the day the stock market had hit a six-week high.

Among the suspects questioned was tennis champion Edwin Fischer, who'd sent postcards to friends warning them to stay away from Wall Street on September 16, information he told F.B.I. agents he'd gotten "out of the air from God." Investigators concluded his prophecy was purely coincidental (it wasn't his first involving the authorities) and committed him to the psychiatric ward at Bellevue. Other suspects reportedly included anarchist newspaper

DESPITE A FOUR-YEAR LONG, MULTI-AGENCY INVESTIGATION, THE PERPETRATORS WERE NEVER IDENTIFIED.

editor Carlo Tresca, watchmaker-electrician Noah Lerner, and union leader "Big Bill" Haywood, who was brought in as a "general precautionary measure," but no evidence was ever found linking any of them to the bombing. Several historians believe that militant Italian anarchist Mario Buda was most likely behind the plot, but Buda (who went by the alias "Mike Boda") was never arrested, despite being in the city at the time of the bombing, and by November was on a ship headed back to his native Naples. Buda allegedly confessed to his role in the bombing to a nephew in 1955, but no evidence was ever uncovered directly implicating him.

Presidential candidate Warren Harding used the attack to stump against "the menace of hyphenated citizenship," warning that control of the country might one day "be

Composite police sketch
of the Wall Street bomber.

Suspect Noah Lerner (center)
at his arraignment in 1923.

transferred to a foreign capital abroad." Even *The Washington Post* jumped on the anti-immigrant bandwagon. "The bomb outrage in New York emphasizes the extent to which the alien scum from the cesspools and sewers of the Old World has polluted the clear spring of American democracy," the paper's editors wrote. "The eradication of foreignism is the outstanding task which America must confront in the next decade."

The editors predicted "a mighty tidal wave by November," and indeed Harding won by a landslide. Soon after his inauguration, he called on Congress to pass legislation restricting immigration, signing the Emergency Quota Act into law on May 19, 1921.

Investigators determined the cart had been packed with 500 pounds of cast-iron sash-window weights and 100 pounds of

dynamite set to a timer. Despite a four-year-long, multi-agency investigation, the perpetrators were never identified. The Department of Justice and the N.Y.P.D. both expanded surveillance of foreign groups after the attack. "This dire catastrophe demonstrates the urgent necessity for a special, or secret, police," wrote Police Commissioner Richard Enright in the department's 1920 annual

Insurance companies wasted no time peddling new "explosion" policies.

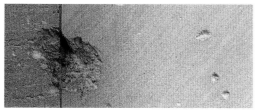

TO THIS DAY, 23 WALL STREET BARES ITS WOUNDS FROM BLOODY THURSDAY.

report, to "maintain a close and unbroken contact with the seditious, anarchistic and dangerously radical elements in this City [who are] thirsting for sensationalism and violence to shore up their insane propaganda and wicked doctrines, and to gain recruits and money through terrorism."

The only employee killed at J. P. Morgan & Company, believed by many to be the intended target of the attack, was a senior clerk in the securities department. The bank's head, J. P. Morgan Jr., was in Europe at the time. He reportedly refused to have the shrapnel pockmarks on the House of Morgan's marble façade filled, as a symbol of defiance against the terrorists and out of respect for the dead. To this day, 23 Wall Street bares its wounds from Bloody Thursday.

19 21

1920–1921

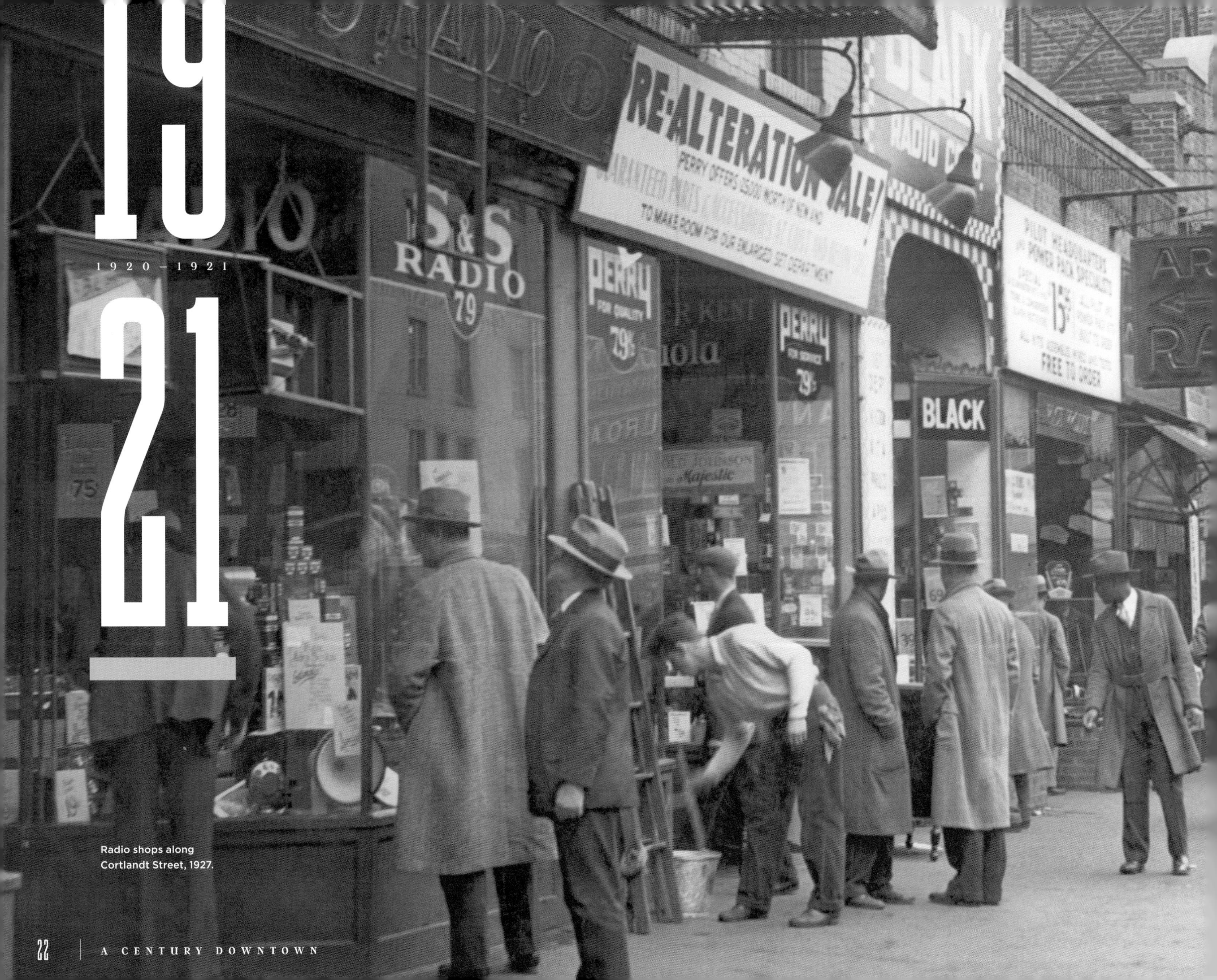

Radio shops along
Cortlandt Street, 1927.

RADIO ROW:
TINKERERS' PARADISE

"To invent, you need a good imagination . . . and a pile of junk."

— THOMAS EDISON

TUBES, KNOBS, TRANSISTORS, transformers, amplifiers, voltmeters, coils, couplers. This was just some of the "junk" enterprising radio buffs could find among the more than 300 electronics shops clustered on and around Lower Manhattan's Cortlandt Street. So endless were the possibilities of finding that elusive tuning-fork oscillator or electrolytic detector that *The New York Times* called the area no less than "a paradise for electronics tinkerers."

B

BUT THERE WASN'T JUST JUNK TO BE HAD. "Here loud-voiced barkers exhort the cash customers not to overlook the wonderful bargains," wrote Robert Hertzberg in the September 1932 issue of *Radio-Craft*, "and at the same time they keep a sharp lookout for the light fingered gentry to whom the low prices mean nothing." Here a well-to-do patron could pick up an ornate Amrad Symphony, a fine walnut-and-brass Stromberg-Carlson Treasure Chest, or an RCA Radiola Grand, the Bentley of 1920s radio cabinets ($4,700 in 2019 dollars). Meanwhile, the less well-heeled could still walk away with a little Philco Midget for a mere 50 cents (seven bucks).

IT WAS *TERRA SIMPATICO,* A MAKERSPACE FOR THE EXCHANGE OF IDEAS AMONG FELLOW RADIOPHILES.

As eclectic as the assorted wares were the shop owners themselves, who hailed from all walks and corners and often branded their businesses eponymously: Blan the Radio Man, Cantor the Cabinet King, Digby Auction, Leotone, Oscar's, Heins and Bolet. (They were neither a subtle nor a modest bunch.) Absent anti-noise regulations at the time, they would compete to lure clientele by blasting everything from opera to big band to step-right-ups from loudspeakers above their entryways, making for a motley cacophony along Cortlandt Street. *The New York Times* called it a "reverberating bedlam [of] musical pandemonium." Eventually "the din was so terrific that the city was forced to pass a municipal ordinance to curb it," according to Hertzberg. Above all the commotion, the whimsical Cortlandt Street "El" station stood stoic watch, like a "Bavarian ski lodge above the street [that] helped give the place the feel of an enclosed bazaar," as James Glanz and Eric Lipton wrote in their seminal history of the World Trade Center, *City in the Sky*.

Harry Schneck was the first to set up shop on Cortlandt when he opened City Radio, in 1921. At the time, the medium was still a novelty. "Most people were intimidated by it," Harry's son, Bill Schneck, recalled on PRX's *Radio Diaries* in 2014. "The idea of information coming through the

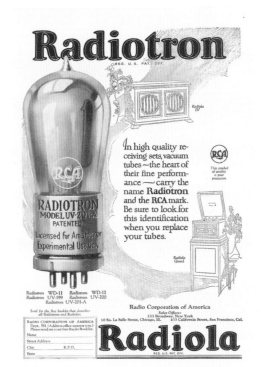

"THE IDEA OF INFORMATION COMING THROUGH THE AIR, THROUGH THE ETHER, WAS ONE STEP AWAY FROM BLACK MAGIC."

Tan, Tough and Terrific!

The "Sportster"

3-way portable radio by

PHILCO

Top Grain Cowhide Case

Every detail, from the "custom look" of the stitching to the richness of that genuine top grain cowhide leather tells you the new Philco 655 is rugged as all outdoors! Handsome durability matched by amazing new "pull-in" power and tone quality. The leather case is specially engineered to snap open for easy changeover from AC-DC to batteries. No portable can touch it at a sensational $39.95*

FREE! *Your* signature in gold on the case.

The "Overnighter"
3-way radio and vanity case in one!

Open the lid—there is your vanity mirror. Then reach into that roomy cosmetic compartment. Holds sun glasses, swim suit, towel, comb... all the items for a girl's outdoor living. Top reception on AC-DC or batteries. Philco 665.

The "First Mate" World's most

powerful 3-Way Marine portable with built-in flashlight. Vital Marine Band services plus standard AM. Long life batteries make it the perfect standby receiver for outboard cruisers. Philco 667.

Hear Johnny Desmond, star of "Philco Phonorama Time" Saturdays 11:30 to 11:55 A.M. Mutual Radio Network

A revelation in realism
from a whisper to a brass band

SCREEN-GRID RADIOLAS
—built by the RCA engineers who created Screen-Grid Radio

RCA Screen-Grid Radiolas in all models give you the superb tone and realism that have made Radiolas a synonym of radio perfection. Why? Because they are built by the RCA experts who created screen-grid and gave it to the radio industry.

Screen-Grid Radiolas are not an experiment. Years were spent in the RCA research laboratories perfecting the Screen-Grid Radiotrons and the special screen-grid circuit which made screen-grid radio possible. RCA engineers then designed a screen-grid set in which interfering foreign noises were eliminated without dulling the high and low notes, and narrowing the musical range.

Tone quality—first essential of fine radio—need not be sacrificed to gain the great advantages of screen-grid. Without tone quality this advanced type of high-power radio is only a makeshift.

When you buy a Screen-Grid Radiola you get super-power screen-grid performance as you have a right to expect it—plus all the qualities of fine radio reception that are guaranteed by the famous RCA trade-mark.

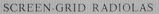

Look for and insist upon the famous RCA trade-mark.

RCA RADIOLA 46—The acknowledged leader in screen-grid "all electric" radio. A cabinet model with built-in RCA electro-dynamic reproducer. For alternating current $150 (less Radiotrons). For direct current $140 (less Radiotrons).

RCA Screen-Grid Radio also in Radiola 44—a compact and beautiful table model, $75 (less Radiotrons).

For those who wish music from the air or record, RCA presents Screen-Grid Radiola 47, the all electric combination of Screen-Grid Radio and Phonograph. $275 (less Radiotrons).

RCA RADIOLA
MADE BY THE MAKERS OF THE RADIOTRON
RADIOLA DIVISION RADIO-VICTOR CORPORATION OF AMERICA

"ONLY A FEW STEPS OFF THE BUSY WATERFRONT, IT IS A MEETING PLACE FOR RADIO OPERATORS FROM ALL OVER THE WORLD."

The view up "Radio Row" toward the Cortlandt Street "El" station, 1930.

air, through the ether, was something that was one step away from black magic." As the shops proliferated, "all of the nuts came out of the woodwork." Within a few years, "Radio Row" was home to the largest concentration of electronics stores in the world, employing some 30,000 workers. Saturday was the big day. Men from all five boroughs and beyond would descend on Cortlandt in multitudes, often with sons (and occasionally daughters) in tow. "On Saturday afternoons it is well nigh impassable," wrote Robert Hertzberg in 1932, "as radio men from the entire metropolitan district come down to do their weekly buying." But it wasn't just buying and selling, hustling and haggling. It was *terra simpatico*, a makerspace for the exchange of ideas among fellow radiophiles: how to fix that temperamental tube, fine-tune a transmitter, build a ham-radio station. "Only a few steps off the busy waterfront, it is a meeting place for radio operators from all over the world," Hertzberg observed. "They often leave souvenirs in the form of tropical fish, South Sea Island shells, Japanese fans, etc., which help to dress up the window displays." Outward chumminess aside, business was business, and the bottom line was the bottom line. "They were all surly," a former Radio Row regular told *Radio Diaries* of the shop owners. "You went there almost for the adventure of being yelled at."

19
21
24

1899–1933

MOTHER COLONY:
LITTLE SYRIA

"THE ENTIRE CITY OF NEW YORK CANNOT SHOW anything more villainously filthy than the old tenements on the west side near the foot of Washington Street, and the dens on their lower floors," wrote Cromwell Childe in the August 20, 1899, issue of *The New York Times Magazine.* "Here hags and heldames gather, wretched old men and great families of dirty children, besides fat matrons and workmen, who do not think it worth the while to wash off the grime of toil." Such was the dim, xenophobic view many took of the burgeoning Syrian community in Lower Manhattan at the turn of the last century. This wasn't the first wave of discrimination, either. "Most of them are devoted to one of two industries," another reporter had cautioned a decade earlier, "thieving and begging. It is time the bars were put up."

The Lebanon Restaurant, 88 Washington Street, 1936.

FOR A NICKEL YOU COULD PICK UP A COPY of the January 24, 1908, issue of the serial *Secret Service: Old and Young King Brady, Detectives.* That week's episode was "The Bradys and the Black Giant; or, The Secrets of 'Little Syria,'" written by "a New-York Detective." "Here are now hived in great numbers Syrians, Arabs, Hindoos and other Asiatic people," wrote the detective. "But about the distinction of nationality the average New Yorker neither knows nor cares. He has chosen to dub this the Syrian quarter, consequently every one who lives there is a Syrian." Syria wasn't yet a nation, so "Syrian" referred to anyone from the expansive territory within the Ottoman Empire that included present-day Syria, Jordan, Lebanon, Israel, and the Palestinian territories.

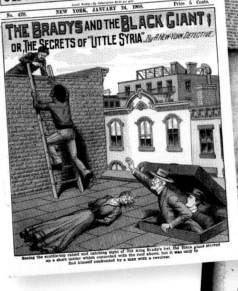

By the early 1920s, Little Syria had nourished a sufficient exchange of goods, ideas, art, and culture to earn it the title "Mother Colony." It had spawned the first Arab-American newspapers and the venerated Pen League, a collective of Middle Eastern writers and poets, including Ameen Rihani, Kahlil Gibran, and Mikhail Naimy, whose "experiments with Western literary forms revolutionized Arabic poetry in the Arab world," as *The Encyclopedia of New York City* duly

Top left: Pen League writers Nasib Arida, Kahlil Gibran, Abdul Massih Haddad, and Mikhail Naimy, 1920.

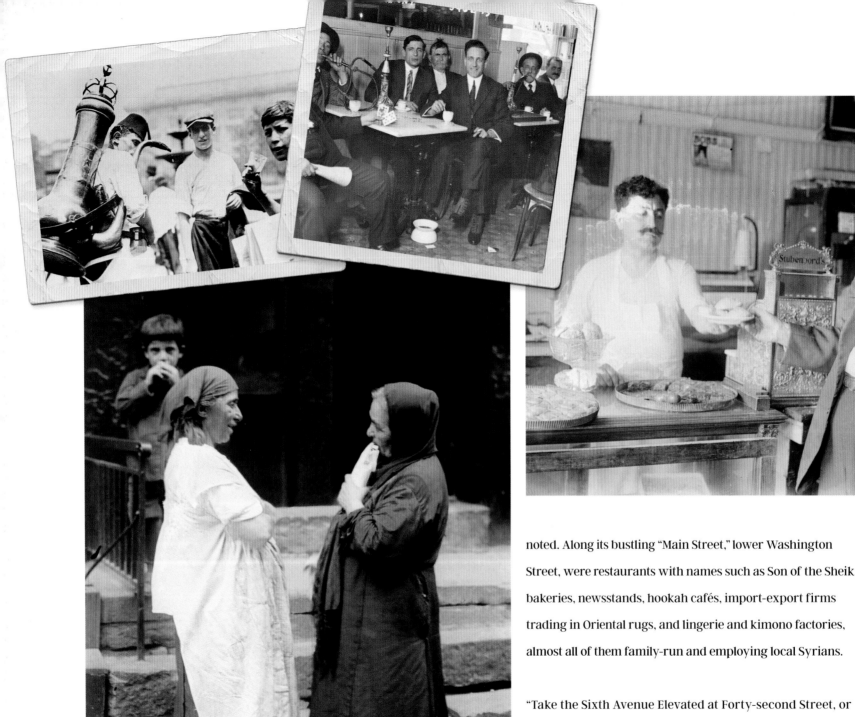

noted. Along its bustling "Main Street," lower Washington Street, were restaurants with names such as Son of the Sheik, bakeries, newsstands, hookah cafés, import-export firms trading in Oriental rugs, and lingerie and kimono factories, almost all of them family-run and employing local Syrians.

"Take the Sixth Avenue Elevated at Forty-second Street, or wherever you happen to be, and in a few minutes you are in Rector Street; walk a block westward to Washington

PASTRY COUNTER — SYRIAN RESTAURANT

Customers buying
markouk bread, 1919.

The well known Restaurant for serving the best of Syrian dishes

Visit the SON OF THE SHEIK, at 77 Washington Street, Iskender Katra, Genial Host

78
MALKO BROS-CASSATL
IMPORTERS & EXPORTERS
of SYRIAN GROCERY
& ORIENTAL ART OBJE

SAHADI'S
EL-AHRAM
BRAND
DELICIOUS
FOOD
NET CONTENTS 15 OUNCES
REG. U.S.
PAT. OFF.
No. 270
No. 510
Class 46
CONTAINS
GROUND SESAME SEEDS
CORN SYRUP
CANE SUGAR
EGG ALBUMEN
FLAVOR BERGAMOO
"IT MELTS IN YOUR MOUTH"
HALWAH

Street and you are in Syria," wrote Romanian-American author Konrad Bercovici in his 1924 book, *Around the World in New York*. "A descent upon the Syrian quarter is like a dream travel." Bercovici described the inhabitants of Little Syria as a "people from a different world, Christians with Moslem habits ... living pell-mell and crowded in tottering old brick houses, a people of a different seed, of an older civilization that has ever been reluctant to the new, distilling a certain pigment into the dull grayness of our modern lives."

BY THE EARLY 1920s, LITTLE SYRIA HAD NOURISHED A SUFFICIENT EXCHANGE OF GOODS AND IDEAS TO EARN IT THE TITLE "MOTHER COLONY."

19 29

1926–1930

Bankrupt investor
Walter Thornton
trying to sell his
luxury roadster,
October 30, 1929.

$100. WILL
BUY THIS CAR.
MUST HAVE CASH.
LOST ALL ON THE
STOCK MARKET

When I listened to the ticker tick
I figured I could get rich quick
But the bunch of bears were too darn slick
My stock come tumblin' down

— LYRIC FROM ARTHUR FIELDS AND FRED HALL'S 1929
SONG "WHEN MY STOCKS COME TUMBLING DOWN"

BLACK TUESDAY

19

FORCED TO SELL ALL HOLDINGS UNLESS RECEIVE CHECK FOR $15,000 TO COVER MARGINS, the ominous telegram read. Its recipient was comedian Harpo Marx, who was in Pittsburgh playing a show with his brothers Groucho, Chico, and Zeppo on October 24, 1929. The sender was Harpo's stockbroker back in New York, who'd sent the panicked message earlier in the day as the market plunged. It reluctantly recovered, but only after five of the country's most powerful bankers intervened. So wild was the ride, even the ticker-tape machines fell behind by as much as four hours. Harpo promptly wired the money to his broker.

B

BUT THE NEXT MORNING HARPO'S BROKER
sent another urgent request. Then another. The final
telegram read, SEND $10,000 IN 24 HOURS OR FACE
FINANCIAL RUIN. "Once worth $250,000 on paper,"
wrote Edward Robb Ellis in *The Epic of New York City*,
"Harpo was almost penniless." Groucho's fortune, too,
had been annihilated. "The jig is up," his broker told
him. "I would have lost more," Groucho later joked,
"but that was all I had." (The brothers had been so
infected with stock-trading fever that they once kept
an audience waiting while they tried to buy up shares
of soaring Anaconda Copper stock.) "He didn't have

"I WOULD HAVE LOST MORE,"
GROUCHO JOKED, "BUT THAT WAS ALL I HAD."

The 40-year-old Harpo, at right, lost $250,000 ($3.6 million in 2019 dollars) in the span of a few days.

a clue what was happening," historian Maury Klein told NPR in 2009. "He didn't know why the prices went up when they did." By Tuesday, October 29, the market had shed 25 percent of its value, wiping out more than $25 billion in supposed wealth.

"In the domestic field there is tranquility and contentment," President Calvin Coolidge had written in his sixth annual message to Congress, on December 4, 1928, "and the highest record of years of prosperity." The Dow Jones Industrial Average jumped 50 percent, topping out at 381 points on September 3, 1929, after having quadrupled over the previous five years. It was the greatest bull market Wall Street had ever seen. "New York City alone had more automobiles than all of Europe," wrote Robb Ellis. "Fifth Avenue's opulence was

Five months after this photograph was taken, Mayor Walker was forced to resign when what *The New York Times* called "the greatest investigation of municipal corruption in American history" revealed he'd taken huge bribes and kickbacks while in office.

rivaled only by Park Avenue, where apartment rentals of $40,000 were not uncommon." By 1929, the top 1 percent held more than 40 percent of the nation's wealth (a figure not to be surpassed until 2017).

Debonair mayor Jimmy Walker embodied the opulence and extravagance of the era. "To high-living, free-spending New Yorkers," wrote Robb Ellis, "Jimmy Walker became a symbol of their way of life." Of his freewheeling spending, Walker once said, "If I earn a million dollars this year, by the end of the year I'd have spent one million, ten thousand." More affectionately known to his constituency as Beau James, he embraced his role as the "Nightclub Mayor," rarely rising before 10 A.M., often hungover. In his first two years in office he took seven vacations—to London, Paris, Rome, Berlin, and Bermuda, among

Above: Men arriving at a party in spats and tails, September 1923.

A socialite getting into her chauffeured Bentley, December 1926.

"NEW YORK CITY ALONE HAD MORE AUTOMOBILES THAN EUROPE."

IT WASN'T JUST SPECULATORS LIKE THE MARX BROTHERS
WHO LOST THEIR SHIRTS ON BLACK TUESDAY.

others—totaling 143 days. He was a throwback to the old "Boss" Tweed–Tammany Hall machine, but New Yorkers didn't seem to mind and re-elected him to a second term in 1929, a week after Black Tuesday.

It wasn't just speculators like the Marx Brothers who lost their shirts. In the aftermath of the Crash, more than nine million savings accounts would evaporate. (It would be another four years until Congress created the F.D.I.C., insuring deposits.) Thousands of banks would fail. Tens of thousands of businesses would go belly-up. Americans would see their incomes cut in half, and a quarter of them would lose their jobs. The vanishing of his fortune triggered a lifelong insomnia in Groucho. But in spite of losing it all on Black Tuesday, the Marx Brothers' fortunes would soon rise again, in a thriving Hollywood during the Great Depression.

A group of Wall Street messenger boys reading the news on October 24, 1929, when the market first showed signs of serious trouble.

19
31

1875 – 1931

THE RISE AND
FALL OF NEWSPAPER ROW

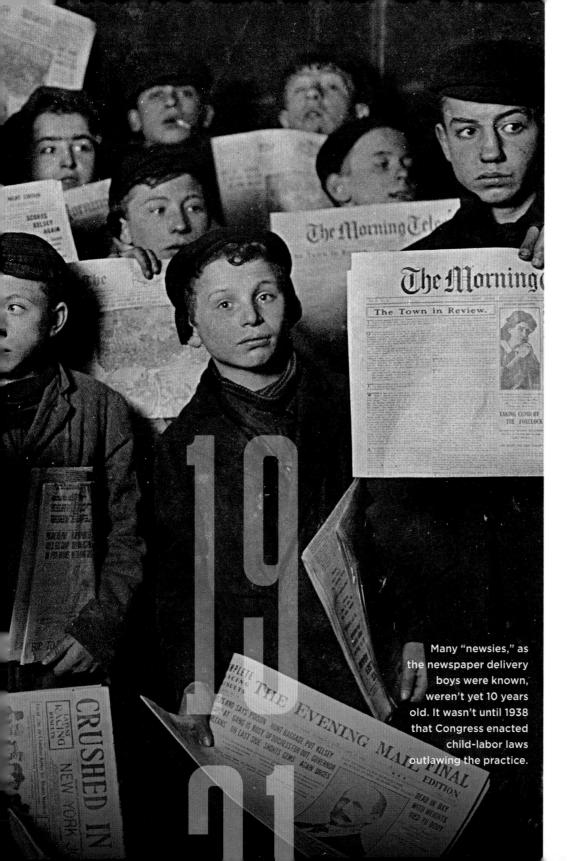

Many "newsies," as the newspaper delivery boys were known, weren't yet 10 years old. It wasn't until 1938 that Congress enacted child-labor laws outlawing the practice.

AS WORKERS ON THE OVERNIGHT "LOBSTER SHIFT" reported for duty at the *World's* headquarters at 53–63 Park Row at midnight on February 27, 1931, they were greeted by the newspaper's editor, H. S. Pollard, who informed them that the printing presses had been shut down. For good. That evening's edition would be the venerable publication's last. "Dear Sir or Madam: You are hereby notified that your employment by the Press Publishing Company is terminated as of February 28, 1931," read the letter sent to all 2,300 employees the next day. "You are to receive two weeks' compensation beyond the specified date." Not welcome news in the depths of the Great Depression, when nearly a quarter of New Yorkers were out of work. Breadlines snaked around the city's blocks. Tens of thousands of homeless inhabited parks, sidewalks, and subways.

T

THE HEYDAY OF "NEWSPAPER ROW" had begun a half-century before, when the leading broadsheets were competing to be the biggest, strongest, and tallest, their rivalry manifesting in the arms race reaching skyward along Park Row. When it opened in 1875, the Tribune Building was taller than anything else in the city, save for the tip of Trinity Church's ornate spire. No less immodest, *The New York Times*'s massive, new granite-and-limestone-clad Romanesque fortress—built around its old 1858 headquarters so as not to interrupt essential newspaper operations—opened at 41 Park Row in 1889. Its five thundering printing presses in the basement were capable of rolling out 12,000 papers an hour. A year later, the *World* moved into its colossal new George B. Post–designed, copper-dome-topped headquarters next door to the

The *World* cost a penny at the turn of the last century, and its circulation was 1.5 million daily readers. "Circulation Books Open to All," it declared—twice, curiously—at the top of the front page.

Left: Joseph Pulitzer, publisher of the *World*, 1900.

"NEWSPAPER ROW OF THE DAY WAS POPULATED BY REDOUBTABLE FIGURES WHO WROTE NOBLE, SHAKESPEARE-TINTED PROSE ABOUT ROUTINE FIRES OR EDITED COPY WITH DIMINISHING WHISKEY BOTTLE CLOSE AT HAND." — ALLEN CHURCHILL, *PARK ROW*

Keystone View Company. Manufacturers and Publishers.

Meadville, Pa., St. Louis, Mo. Copyright 1903, by B. L. Singley.

13500—City Hall and World Building, New York, N. Y., U. S. A.

Tammany Hall corruption would be duly exposed by the reporters across Printing House Square.

"A glaring collocation of red and white and black, which time can never mellow," wrote the *World*'s architecture critic Montgomery Schuyler of the Tribune Building.

BY 1931, NEARLY A QUARTER OF NEW YORKERS WERE OUT OF WORK. MORE THAN 60,000 WERE HOMELESS.

Tribune. For the next four years, it was the tallest building in the world. From his office in the dome, the self-made Hungarian-immigrant publisher, Joseph Pulitzer, could gaze down on his competitors to the south; City Hall to the west; and the Brooklyn Bridge, not yet a decade old, to the east.

"As important as the architecture was the site: facing down City Hall," wrote *New York Times* reporter David Dunlap in 2001. "It was a declaration that the newspaper regarded itself as a powerful institution in civic life. ... No politician standing on the broad steps of City Hall could fail to note the newspaper's presence." And indeed Tammany Hall's corrupt bosses would be duly exposed by the battalions of dogged gumshoe-reporters filing in and out of the skyscrapers across Printing House Square daily.

The *Tribune's* copy editors worked in the building's sunlit upper floors.

The circulation battles between rival newspapers gave rise to the term "yellow journalism," whose practitioners relied on sensationalism and brazen headlines to sell papers.

By 1931, the *World* was Newspaper Row's sole holdout. In 1894, the *Herald* had been the first to migrate uptown, to what would soon become known as Herald Square, a nod to the rank of newspapers in the city's civic hierarchy at the time. Ditto the *Times*, which decamped to "Times Square" in 1904. The *Tribune* merged with the *Herald* in 1924 and eventually moved out, too.

After a newsstand-price hike triggered a decline in circulation, Pulitzer's heirs were eager to unload their father's legacy. A provision in his will prohibited the *World*'s sale, but a generous Surrogate's Court judge approved transfer to the Scripps-Howard chain, owner of dozens of newspapers nationwide, on February 26, 1931. Scripps-Howard merged its *Telegram* with the *World* to spawn the *New York World-Telegram* (which would itself eventually shutter in 1966). "Everybody I knew who ever worked on The World was proud to have done so," wrote Joel Sayre in the *Times* in 1974. "It lent a mark of distinction, rather the way having served in the Marine Corps is supposed to do." From its reigning perch atop Times Square, the *Times* seemed to revel in the *World*'s—and Newspaper Row's—eventual demise. PARK ROW'S NEWSPAPER GLORY FADES OUT WITH THE WORLD, the *Times*'s headline announced a day after the *World-Telegram* merger. The article read, "The passing of The World marks the end of 'Newspaper Row,' as Park Row was called when nearly every important newspaper was printed downtown."

The New York World Building was demolished in 1955 to make way for automobile on-ramps to the Brooklyn Bridge. The Tribune Building was torn down by Pace University in 1966. The New York Times Building at 41 Park Row (far right) is the only surviving structure from Newspaper Row.

"AS IMPORTANT AS THE ARCHITECTURE WAS THE SITE: FACING DOWN CITY HALL."

— DAVID DUNLAP, *THE NEW YORK TIMES*, 2001

19

1940–1950

40

PRESIDENT VS. POWER BROKER

"I FEEL LIKE SAYING TODAY, 'AT LAST,' because for some time there was some dispute as to whether we would cross the East River between Manhattan and Brooklyn under the water or over the water," President Franklin D. Roosevelt told a few thousand invited guests at a groundbreaking ceremony in Red Hook, Brooklyn, on October 28, 1940. "And they told us— the Army Engineers—looking way, way into the future, we hope so far away that none of us will live to see it, there might be an attack on America, and if that attack were to come it would be safer for America and all its cities if we could have this tunnel instead of that bridge."

A photographic rendering of the proposed Brooklyn-Battery bridge, 1939.

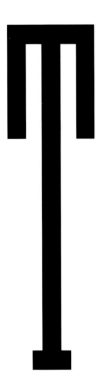

THE COST OF THE TUNNEL was projected at $81 million, but Roosevelt assured the politicians present, including the mayor, the governor, and other top officials, that the tunnel would eventually "pay itself out" from the tolls it collected. With that, he "pulled a cord attached to the whistle of a steam shovel," reported *The New York Times*, "and as the signal sounded, Louis Cappola, operator of the shovel—a crane type—dropped the great steel 'bucket,' opened its jaws, took a big bite of earth, and dumped the soil into a ten-ton truck."

President Franklin D. Roosevelt in the Oval Office, December 1941.

It would have been hard to overstate the extent to which President Roosevelt and Robert Moses, then chairman of the Triborough Bridge Authority, held each other in contempt. Moses was no mere bureaucrat running a bridge authority; he was New York City's fabled and feared "Master Builder" and "Power Broker," responsible for the Whitestone and Triborough Bridges, Jones Beach, hundreds of playgrounds, and nearly a dozen enormous public swimming pools, among other popular projects. Few and far between were politicians willing to cross him.

Roosevelt and Moses had been feuding as far back as 1924, when the two clashed over funding for the Taconic State Parkway. (Roosevelt was then chairman of the Taconic State Park Commission; Moses was president of the Long Island State Park Commission.) Now Moses wanted another soaring bridge—not an unsightly tunnel—to connect Brooklyn to Lower Manhattan, and he was determined to prevail over his old nemesis, now president of the United States.

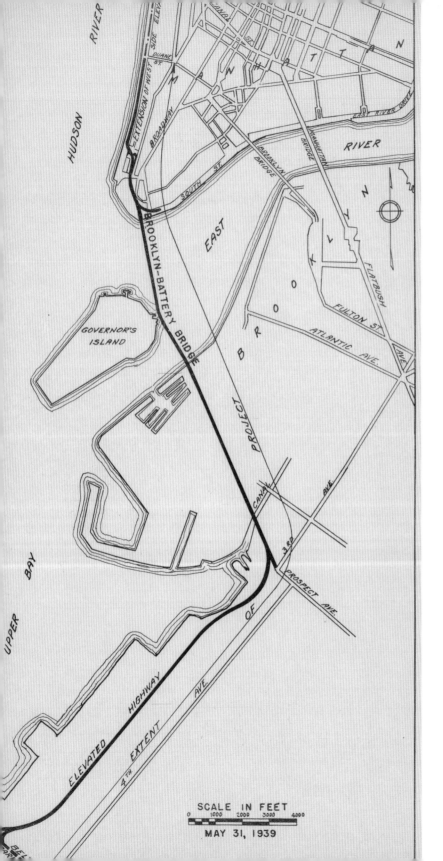

SCALE IN FEET
0 1000 2000 3000 4000

MAY 31, 1939

But the Power Broker met his match as community groups, civic leaders, historic preservationists, Wall Street executives, and the mayor and the governor, not to mention friends of the New York Aquarium at Castle Garden—which would have been demolished to make way for the bridge—closed ranks in opposition to his imperious plan. "A bridge with its terminus and approaches at the Battery will seriously disfigure perhaps the most thrillingly beautiful and world-renowned feature of this great city," wrote one opposition group.

But it was ultimately the secretary of war Harry Woodring, who intervened, scuttling Moses's bridge because it was "seaward of a vital naval establishment," the Brooklyn Navy Yard. Reportedly out of spite, Moses took retaliatory aim at the aquarium, one of the city's most popular attractions, shuttering it on the dubious grounds that construction of the tunnel would undermine Castle Garden's fragile foundation.

"A BRIDGE WILL SERIOUSLY DISFIGURE PERHAPS THE MOST THRILLINGLY BEAUTIFUL AND WORLD-RENOWNED FEATURE OF THIS GREAT CITY."

822 AQUARIUM, FORMERLY CASTLE GARDEN,
AND WHITEHALL BLDG., NEW YORK

Images of Castle Garden
and the New York Aquarium,
circa 1893–1936.

The last remnants of Little Syria were demolished in the early 1940s to make way for the entrance ramps to the tunnel. "Expediting auto traffic to suburbia took priority over the community of politically powerless city dwellers," New York University professor Jack Tchen wrote in his 2002 essay, "Whose Downtown?!?" "The Syrians had to leave and restart their businesses and their lives somewhere else."

"Most [Little Syria] residents were Christian, their loyalties divided only between St. George's Syrian Catholic Church at 103 Washington Street and St. Joseph's Maronite Church at 57 Washington Street," wrote *The New York Times*'s David Dunlap in 2012. St. George's is one of just three remaining buildings from the days of Little Syria and was declared an official landmark in 2009 by the city's Landmarks Preservation Commission. "It remains Lower Manhattan's most vivid reminder of the vanished ethnic community once known as the Syrian Quarter," wrote the commission in its report, "and of the time when Washington Street was the Main Street of Syrian America."

"EXPEDITING AUTO TRAFFIC TO SUBURBIA TOOK PRIORITY OVER THE COMMUNITY OF POLITICALLY POWERLESS CITY DWELLERS."

Groundbreaking ceremony for the Brooklyn-Battery Tunnel, October 28, 1940, in Red Hook, Brooklyn.

An elevation drawing of St. George's Syrian Catholic Church at 103 Washington Street, 1929. The building was landmarked in 2009.

1041

WASHINGTON MARKET

Washington Market sat directly beneath what is today's One World Trade Center, occupying an entire block from West to Washington Streets, and from Vesey to Fulton. To the south was Radio Row, home to the biggest concentration of electronics shops in the world.

WASHINGTON MARKET

19 41

1 8 1 2 — 1 9 6 2

"NEW YORK'S GREAT CROSSROADS OF VEGETABLES," as a local public-radio host once called it, "dates back to when water actually flowed through Canal Street." A Lower Manhattan institution for a century and a half, the steadfast—some would say stubborn—Washington Market went through several incarnations in its long life, occupying the same city block bounded by Washington, West, Fulton, and Vesey Streets, from a ramshackle bevy of sheds and pushcarts to a vast "modern" refrigerated hall with hundreds of vendor stalls.

"An epicurean wonderland that makes the biggest and best gastro-mall anywhere today look like fingerling potatoes."
— E D I B L E   M A N H A T T A N ,   2 0 1 0

"AS YOU WALKED ALONG, dodging hand trucks, ducking down corridors of crated watercress, you were startled and delighted by the smells," recalled James Stevenson in the March 16, 1968, issue of *The New Yorker,* "so strange in New York, where most smells are from something thrown out, burned up, dead, or rotting." Washington Market was an aromatic oasis, a refuge from the city's daily stench, full of enticing scents that were "sharp and clean" from "freshness and life." At its peak, more than 500 vendors sold whatever genus of fresh produce one could possibly conjure, not to mention "caviar from Siberia, Gorgonzola cheese from Italy, hams from Flanders, sardines from Norway, English partridge, native quail, squabs, wild ducks and pheasants," according to the 1939 *WPA Guide to New York City.* From two A.M. to six A.M.,

WASHINGTON MARKET WAS AN AROMATIC OASIS, A REFUGE FROM THE CITY'S DAILY STENCH.

Butchers unload meat from a refrigerated truck, 1945.

Imagine traveling back in time and trying to explain to one of Washington Market's gruff vendors that one day on this very spot would rise a 1,776-foot-tall glass-and-steel "Freedom Tower."

vendors wholesaled exclusively to grocers and restaurateurs but opened for everyone else the rest of the day.

By midcentury, Washington Market had begun to fall out of favor in a rapidly changing downtown. Congressman George M. Grant, chairman of a House subcommittee investigating food markets nationwide, derided its "horse and buggy facilities," woefully inadequate "for the biggest perishable food market in the world," where 10 percent of the country's foodstuffs were exchanged. "It is hard to believe," he remarked after a visit to the market in 1949, "that we will find anything worse than that here in New York." In 1958, the city put the Washington Market building up for auction, but no bidders were forthcoming. Within a decade, it had shuttered and relocated to a new facility in Hunts Point, the Bronx.

"We knew that the Market was being torn down, but we didn't realize how fast until we went there one morning last week,"

James Stevenson noted in 1968. "Entire blocks of buildings along Washington Street and Greenwich Street had vanished, leaving what looked like fields growing crops of brick." The adjacent Radio Row had already been razed. In all, 13 full blocks were bulldozed to make way for the new "World Trade Center" complex. At its apex, Washington Market had been likened to Paris's grand, iconic Les Halles food bazaar. But no matter what city you're in, the march of urban progress takes no prisoners. Les Halles itself would be demolished in 1971 to make way for the Forum des Halles shopping mall and transit hub.

NO MATTER WHAT CITY YOU'RE IN, THE MARCH OF URBAN PROGRESS TAKES NO PRISONERS.

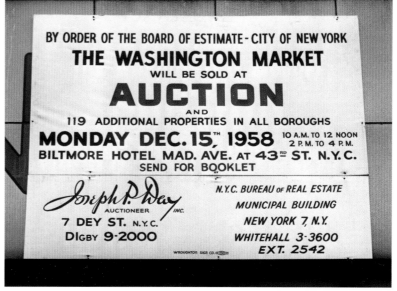

19
45

1886 – 1969

I LIKE IKE

CANYON OF HEROES

"I LIKE IKE" is how General Dwight Eisenhower's presidential-campaign slogan would read a few years later, but by the turnout for his ticker-tape parade, on June 19, 1945, it was clear plenty of folks already quite liked Ike. As supreme commander of the Allied Expeditionary Force in the European theater during World War II, Eisenhower had led the Allies to victory, earning pop-hero status and setting the stage for an unprecedented era of American prosperity and global expansion.

FRANK LESLIE'S ILLUSTRATED NEWSPAPER

No 1,624.—Vol. LXIII.]   NEW YORK—FOR THE WEEK ENDING NOVEMBER 6, 1886.   [PRICE, 10 CENTS.

NEW YORK CITY.—THE GRAND DEMONSTRATION ON "LIBERTY DAY," OCTOBER 28TH.—THE MILITARY AND CIVIC PROCESSION PASSING DOWN LOWER BROADWAY, WITH THE NAVAL PAGEANT IN THE DISTANCE.

FROM A SKETCH BY A STAFF ARTIST.—SEE PAGE 162.

ON OCTOBER 28, 1886, New York City celebrated the dedication of the Statue of Liberty, a gift from France, with a sweeping parade that stretched from 55th and Fifth to the Battery. French and American flags adorned the route. Onlookers clambered atop wagons, stood on flower barrels, and hung out of windows to get a glimpse. The crowds grew denser and more feverish as the parade wormed its way south. When the procession of Grand Army veterans, firemen, dignitaries, politicians, and other notables reached Broadway and Wall Street, thin ribbons of paper spontaneously began to float down from the stone canyon walls above.

"All this display was an inspiration to so many imps of office boys, who, from a hundred windows began to unreel the spools of tape that record the fateful messages of the 'ticker,'" reported *The New York Times*. "In a moment the air was white with curling streamers." As the parade neared the Battery, the wind blowing off the harbor swirled the paper swarm into a blizzard. "Hundreds caught in the meshes of electric wires and made a snowy canopy, and others floated downward and were caught by the crowd." And so the ticker-tape parade was born.

Left: 25-year-old Charles Lindbergh became a global media sensation after making the first solo nonstop transatlantic flight, in 1927.

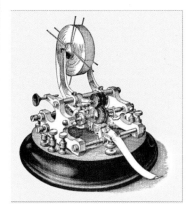

Various models of
stock-ticker machines,
vintage 1873–1935.

BY THE TURN OF THE LAST CENTURY, THOUSANDS OF TICKERS WERE UNSPOOLING STOCK SYMBOLS INTO OFFICES ALL AROUND DOWNTOWN.

The first ticker-tape machine was invented by Western Union's chief telegrapher, Edward A. Calahan, in 1867. Until then, Wall Street had relied on "pad shovers," long-legged young messengers who literally ran stock prices from trading floors to brokers and bankers, but Calahan's new machine offered nearly instantaneous dissemination of market data via telegraph wire. He sold the patent for the then immense sum of $100,000 to the Gold & Stock Telegraph Co., where an ambitious 23-year-old named Thomas Edison improved on Calahan's design, patenting

JUNE 20, 1932   **AMELIA EARHART**   EARHART WAS FÊTED FOR BEING THE FIRST WOMAN TO FLY SOLO ACROSS THE ATLANTIC.

SEPT. 3, 1936

**JESSE
OWENS**

THE CHAMPION HAD WON FOUR GOLD MEDALS IN TRACK
AND FIELD AT THE 1936 SUMMER OLYMPICS IN BERLIN.

OCT. 19, 1960

J.F.K. AND JACKIE

SENATOR JOHN F. KENNEDY AND WIFE, JACQUELINE, DREW AN ENTHUSIASTIC CROWD. LESS THAN A MONTH LATER, KENNEDY WOULD WIN THE U.S. PRESIDENTIAL ELECTION.

MARCH 1, 1962

JOHN GLENN

ASTRONAUT JOHN GLENN WAS HONORED AFTER
BECOMING THE FIRST AMERICAN TO ORBIT THE EARTH.

OCT. 20, 1969

**THE
METS**

THE WORLD SERIES CHAMPION NEW YORK
METS SLOWLY MADE THEIR WAY UP BROADWAY
TO A WARM WELCOME AT CITY HALL.

his own Universal Stock Printer in 1871. By the turn of the last century, thousands of tickers were unspooling stock symbols into offices all around downtown.

The frequency of ticker-tape parades surged after the Second World War: 130 of the city's 206 parades happened in the two decades following Ike's grand fêting. They saluted generals, admirals, commanders, veterans, prime ministers, mayors, presidents, sports champions, firemen, musicians, aviators, and astronauts. By the early 1960s, ticker tape had become obsolete, displaced by electronic displays. (Taking its place would be a confetti medley of shredded office paper and toilet tissue.) The frequency of parades declined sharply beginning in the 1970s—less than two dozen were held between 1970 and 2015—much to the relief of the city's Sanitation Department, whose workers sometimes had to sweep up more than a thousand tons of debris after the blockbuster parades of the 1960s.

Brooms and dump trucks would eventually give way to mechanical sweepers and leaf blowers, making for much quicker cleanups after parades.

BY THE EARLY 1960s, TICKER TAPE HAD BECOME OBSOLETE.

"Any man with a good pair of lungs is free to trade there so long as he keeps good his contracts."
—*The New York Times*, 1908

THE CURB MARKET

"IT TEARS CONTROL OF A GOLD-MINE FROM AN UNLUCKY OPERATOR, AND PAUSES
TO AUCTION A PUPPY-DOG," WROTE EDWIN C. HILL IN *MUNSEY'S* MAGAZINE IN 1920.
"IT IS LIKE NOTHING ELSE UNDER THE ASTONISHING SKY THAT IS ITS ONLY ROOF."
THE NEW YORK CURB MARKET, WHICH OPERATED ON A STRETCH OF BROAD STREET,
RAIN OR SHINE, WAS A PETRI DISH OF EMERGING ENTERPRISES SEEKING SPECULATIVE
CAPITAL, AND THE MINOR LEAGUE FOR YOUNG STOCK AND BOND TRADERS FROM
ALL WALKS BENT ON ONE DAY MAKING IT TO THE "BIG EXCHANGE." MANY WERE
THE WELL-HEELED SONS OF BANKERS, WHOSE PROMINENT FATHERS HAD SENT THEM
TO WORK ON THE CURB "TO GAIN THROUGH HARD KNOCKS A FOUNDATION
KNOWLEDGE OF THE PRACTICAL WORKINGS OF FINANCE," ACCORDING TO HILL, WHILE
OTHERS WERE OUTER-BOROUGH "OFFICE-BOYS, QUICK-WITTED AND FIRED BY ZEAL
TO GET AHEAD." AMONG THE COMPANIES WHOSE STOCKS TRADED ON THE CURB—
BEFORE THEY GRADUATED TO THE NEW YORK STOCK EXCHANGE—WERE STANDARD
OIL, COCA-COLA, AND GENERAL MOTORS.

By 1921, the curb brokers had cobbled together enough money to put a roof over their heads, building a neo-Renaissance-style trading hall designed by Starrett & Van Vleck.

1953

*"Finance set
to jazz music."*

In 1930, the Curb Market added a 14-story Art Deco tower on Trinity Place, and in 1953 rebranded itself as the American Stock Exchange.

59

THE BANKERS CLUB

Top right: The club's
Lounging Room, 1915.
Right: The club's marble-
walled main lobby.

"The largest lunching club ever attempted."

— *ARCHITECTURE AND BUILDING MAGAZINE, MAY 1915*

"THE KEYNOTE OF THE CLUB IS BIGNESS," *The New York Times* noted when the exclusive Bankers Club of America opened on the top three floors of the Equitable Building in July 1915. Its board of governors included "fifty-two of the best-known men of the city in banking, business and legal circles." Membership was capped at 1,500. Within a few years, the Great War was over and Wall Street had assumed the mantle of financial capital of the world from London's Square Mile. The Roaring Twenties followed, giving birth to the Jazz Age, Art Deco, and organized crime. As the stock market soared and Prohibition took hold, bankers and bootleggers alike struck gold.

O

OVER THE NEXT 64 YEARS, the Bankers Club would host dignitaries— Charles de Gaulle, Winston Churchill, Nikita Khrushchev, Queen Elizabeth II, to name a few—and a dozen U.S. presidents, who might have enjoyed a main course of fresh seafood from the nearby Fulton Fish Market in one of the club's mahogany-paneled dining rooms, afterwards sinking into one of the plush red leather chairs next to the marble fireplace in the stately Lounging Room.

The club sat squarely at the intersection of politics and Wall Street and was a vital presidential-campaign fund-raising stop. "When Presidents' needs were financial (and each President has had such needs)," according to the *Times*, "they met with Wall Street's elite in an intimate room reserved for them." It was also a place where big ideas could be discreetly pitched to the lords of high finance. "I firmly believe that the next few years will witness a truly remarkable series of accomplishments in the redevelopment of this historic section of New York City," Chase Manhattan Bank's David Rockefeller told a roomful of elites on October 8, 1959, before introducing his plan for a "World Trade Center" downtown.

Designed by the firm of E. R. Graham, the neoclassical Equitable Building became the biggest—if not the tallest— skyscraper in the world when it opened in early 1915, occupying an entire city block at 120 Broadway. The outcry from

The Bankers Club of America

EQUITABLE BUILDING.
120 BROADWAY, NEW YORK

June 26th, 1915.

The Bankers Club of America will open on Thursday, July 1st.

The Board of Governors invites your representative to be its guest on Wednesday afternoon, June 30th, between the hours of four and seven.

Refreshments will be served.

R. S. V. P. TO
GEORGE T. WILSON
VICE-PRESIDENT
120 BROADWAY, NEW YORK

THE PILGRIMS

LUNCHEON IN HONOR OF

THE RIGHT HONORABLE

The EARL of LYTTON
K.G., G.C.S.I., G.C.I.E.

FORMERLY GOVERNOR OF BENGAL. CHAIRMAN
OF THE LEAGUE OF NATIONS MISSION TO
MANCHURIA

THE BANKERS CLUB OF AMERICA

neighbors, whose sunlight had been almost entirely cut off by the behemoth, was resounding. "The Equitable became the prime example cited of the evils of unregulated skyscraper construction," the Landmarks Preservation Commission noted before designating it a city landmark in 1996, and "has been considered the single most important building affecting the development and passage of New York's zoning law, the first in the country." While it didn't impose height restrictions, the city's 1916 Zoning Resolution limited new buildings to a percentage of lot size, mandating a modicum of sunlight reach

BANKERS AND BOOTLEGGERS ALIKE STRUCK GOLD.

the surrounding canyons. The result was a decades-long proliferation of "wedding cake" towers with "stepped façades." The zoning law was revised in 1961, encouraging developers to "provide structures with clean lines, open plazas and attractive arcades" in exchange for "floor area bonuses."

"Yesterday an era ended," the *Times* declared on February 2, 1979. "Wall Street has changed, with one of its most prestigious clubs going the way many of its firms have gone in the last few years." The club's board had voted to reject the new lease terms offered by the Equitable Building's owners and chose to fold rather than relocate. By then the club had already lost much of its luster. Many of Wall

THE CLUB SAT SQUARELY AT THE INTERSECTION OF POLITICS AND WALL STREET.

Street's biggest firms had long since migrated uptown, building their own newfangled dining rooms and luxe lounges. A year after the club closed, developer Larry Silverstein bought the Equitable Building for $60 million and immediately set about renovating it, carefully restoring such original details as the terra-cotta window frames and the lobby's Tennessee-pink-marble floor.

In July 2019, Silverstein completed another major restoration of the building—to the tune of $50 million—and reincarnated the Bankers Club on the 40th floor. The new club features 20,000 square feet of landscaped terraces and an 8,000 square foot café and cocktail bar.

Above right: 120 Broadway's recently restored lobby.

Right: Ribbon-cutting ceremony for the new Bankers Club at 120 Broadway, July 17, 2019. From left: AJ Arlauckas, Lisa Bevacqua, Stuart Feinberg, Larry Silverstein, Tal Kerret, Carlos Cardoso, Matt Rich, Bill Dacunto, Joseph Artusa, Jeremy Moss, and Carl Lettich.

"The largest building project since the Egyptian pyramids."

THE BROTHERS ROCKEFELLER

AT A MODEST CEREMONY ON MAY 21, 1939, at the World's Fair in Flushing Meadows, Queens, "a handful of third-tier government officials dutifully raised a flag at the dedication of a rather unpretentious pavilion," James Glanz and Eric Lipton wrote in *City in the Sky.* The idea for a "World Trade Center" pavilion had been hatched only after China pulled out of the fair, leaving its space in the

1961

1 9 3 9 – 1 9 6 2

Far left: A model of the proposed new headquarters of the Chase Manhattan Bank. Left: Posters for the 1939 New York World's Fair.

Hall of Nations vacant and in need of a new tenant. The International Chamber of Commerce stepped in, launching an exhibit dedicated to "world peace through world trade." A lofty notion, sure, but it hardly measured up to the neighboring 610-foot-tall Trylon and its globular conjoined Perisphere, Elektro the Moto-Man and his dog "Sparks," or the wildly popular Futurama ride, which so aptly envisioned the future of the American freeway. It would be another two decades before the "World Trade Center" concept would gain any traction.

C

CHASE NATIONAL BANK MERGED

with the Bank of the Manhattan Company
in early 1955, making urgent the need for
a new headquarters for the nation's now
second-biggest bank, Chase Manhattan.
An ambitious 40-year-old vice president
at the bank named David Rockefeller,
grandson of Standard Oil tycoon John D.
Rockefeller, was tasked with spearheading
the project. A steady migration of firms to
Midtown had left downtown in decline, but
Rockefeller insisted the bank double down

The newly opened
One Chase Manhattan
Plaza, 1961.

A STEADY MIGRATION OF FIRMS TO MIDTOWN HAD LEFT DOWNTOWN IN DECLINE.

on "one of the most valuable and uniquely situated pieces of real estate in the entire world." To promote his vision, he set up the Downtown-Lower Manhattan Association, which lobbied for no less than a wholesale makeover of downtown's aging skyline.

By the end of the year, Rockefeller had announced plans for a sleek 60-story, 813-foot-tall International Style glass-and-aluminum tower designed by Gordon Bunshaft and Jacques Guiton of Skidmore, Owings & Merrill. Construction began at

One Chase Manhattan Plaza towers above the Federal Reserve Bank of New York Building (lower right).

the corner of Liberty and William Streets, the former address of the Mutual Life Insurance Company, in January 1957. Four years later, the new One Chase Manhattan Plaza drew widespread praise, even earning a nod from Ada Louise Huxtable, the tough-as-bolts doyenne of architectural criticism for much of the 20th century. "These are the kind of monumental undertakings that would make a Pharaoh or a Roman Emperor blush," she wrote in *The New York Times*, "and turn the Medici green with envy." Reporter David Dunlap would later call it "the silvery, sky-scraping symbol of Lower Manhattan's emergence into the modern era of architecture and finance."

Rockefeller was emboldened to set his sights even higher on what he called "catalytic bigness," something so big it couldn't be ignored, so overwhelming it would spawn additional development. In June 1959, a few months before One Chase topped out, Rockefeller retained consulting firm McKinsey & Company to study the financial viability of a world trade center downtown, anticipating a rubber stamp. Instead, McKinsey's report cast a dubious shadow over the project, concluding it would be a risky investment and "a long hard pull" to realize. But as negative as the firm's assessment was, it didn't entirely refute Rockefeller's notion of "catalytic bigness," instead assigning the project greater promise if it was "unusual in nature and spectacular in proportions to act as an irresistible magnet to such lukewarm prospective tenants." Rockefeller promptly shelved the report and moved ahead with his plans.

A WORLD CENTER OF TRADE MAPPED OFF WALL STREET, read *The New York Times* headline on January 27, 1960. Rockefeller had pitched his vision of the project to a handful of reporters

McKINSEY'S REPORT CAST A
DUBIOUS SHADOW OVER THE PROJECT.

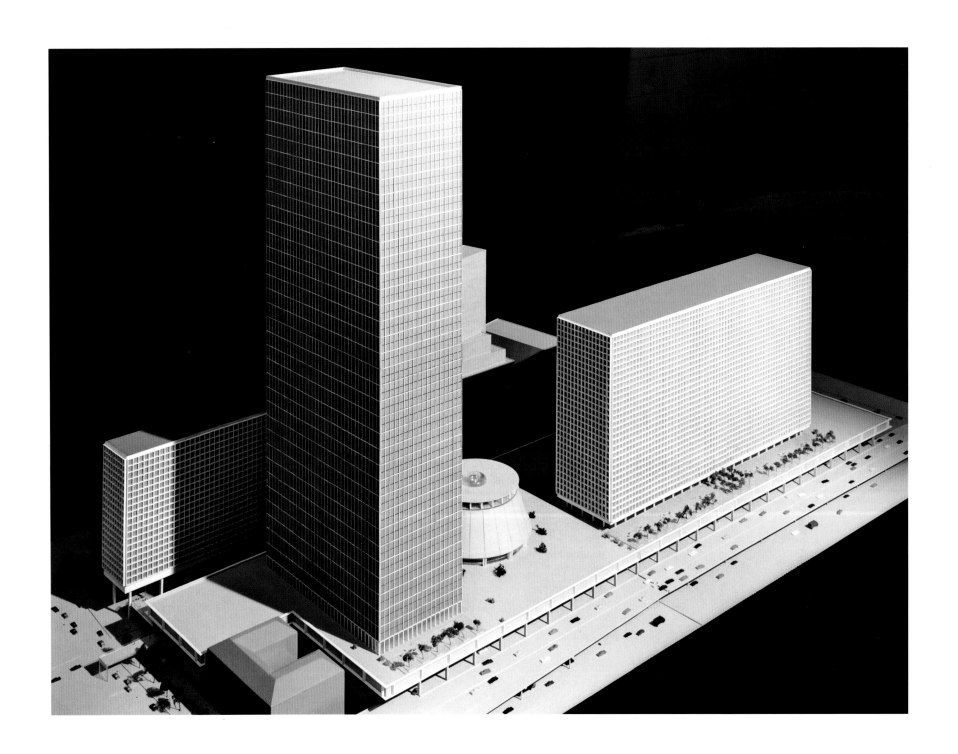

THE PORT AUTHORITY WASN'T IN
THE REAL-ESTATE BUSINESS.

Opposite and above: A model of the original World Trade Center proposal on the East River, 1960.

in a downtown boardroom the day before, excitedly describing a sprawling $250 million complex, spreading from the foot of Wall Street north and south over 13 acres. It would include a 70-story tower, a six-story "international trade mart and exhibition hall," and a "central securities exchange building," to which Rockefeller hoped to lure the New York Stock Exchange.

Catalytic bigness also meant a sky-high price tag that couldn't be funded solely by private interests. David Rockefeller knew a project of such magnitude would need government backing. The Port of New York Authority—the omnipotent bi-state agency that had built many of the region's major bridges, tunnels, airports, and its namesake bus terminal—wasn't in the real-estate business, and its board was wary of Rockefeller's proposal. Undeterred, he pressed on, eventually finding an ally and kindred spirit in the agency's imperious executive director, Austin J. Tobin. It didn't hurt that Rockefeller's brother Nelson had by then been governor of New York for more than a year and had quietly been filling vacant Port Authority board seats with sympathetic appointees.

But New Jersey governor Robert Meyner, who shared control of the Port Authority equally with Governor Rockefeller and their respective state legislatures, was vexed by the remote East River location. "What's in it for me?" he asked Rockefeller after sizing up a model of the complex. New Jersey's bankrupt Hudson & Manhattan Railroad, whose decrepit "Hudson Tubes" connecting Manhattan to Jersey City and Hoboken had long been shedding riders and dollars, was a chronic political headache for Meyner. He saw a bargaining chip in Rockefeller's pitch. Rockefeller and Tobin would get his blessing for their East Side complex if the Port Authority bailed out the railroad, which suffered from "constant service outages and a tumbledown, rat-infested physical plant," as Glanz and Lipton noted.

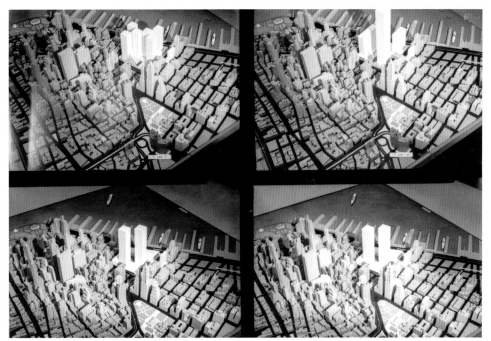

"WHAT'S IN IT FOR ME?"
MEYNER ASKED ROCKEFELLER.

Left: David Rockefeller, artist Marc Chagall, and Governor Nelson Rockefeller at the United Nations. Above: Models of the proposed World Trade Center after it was moved to the West Side.

In the meantime, Tobin and his cadre of urban planners at the Port Authority had already hatched a backup plan. Why not move the World Trade Center to the West Side? If the Port Authority rescued the Hudson & Manhattan Railroad, couldn't it also lay claim to the company's run-down twin 22-story office towers above the railroad's main terminal beneath Church Street, which could be expeditiously razed? (Not as easily condemned would be the surrounding Radio Row neighborhood.) The West Side plan was privately pitched to New Jersey's governor-elect Richard Hughes in December 1961. "I think I can sell that," Hughes replied. Within three months, he and Governor Rockefeller had signed a bill green-lighting the project, which would soon grow to 16 acres and 10 million square feet of office space, more than in all of Houston or Detroit. The brothers Rockefeller would get their catalytic World Trade Center and New Jersey would get its renovated Hudson Tubes—rebranded as the Port Authority Trans-Hudson (PATH) line—which would deposit New Jersey commuters in a brand-new terminal directly beneath it.

19
62

RADIO PARADISE LOST

BUSINESS SLUMPED DURING THE SECOND WORLD WAR, but Radio Row rebounded as surplus military equipment flooded the market. Then came frequency-modulation radio (FM) and, later, color television. By the early 1960s, the shops along Cortlandt Street were moving not just an abundance of "brown goods" (radios and TVs) but "white goods" (refrigerators, washers, dryers) too. Despite the turnaround, the neighborhood's days would be numbered. On March 27, 1962, the governors of New York and New Jersey announced plans for the "World Trade Center," to be built smack-dab on Radio Row.

SE HABLA ESPANOL
ARMY & NAVY GOODS

19
1962 – 1967
62

A crowd huddles outside the entrance to Morel's Electronics, on Washington Street, listening to the news of President John F. Kennedy's assassination, November 22, 1963.

SHOP OWNERS CLOSED RANKS and, led by the inimitable Oscar Nadel of Oscar's Radio, sued the Port Authority and took to the streets. In one of the more memorable protests—a mock funeral procession—Nadel was carried up and down Cortlandt Street in a makeshift coffin while giving interviews to reporters, flanked by supporters clutching placards with slogans like "Don't Let P.A. Kill Mr. Small Businessman."

"NO HOME OR BUSINESS IS SAFE FROM THE CAPRICE OF GOVERNMENT."

"THERE WERE A LOT OF BROKEN MEN."

"This is not some foreign country where the government can come in and just take a man's business," he told a *New York Times* reporter. The shop owners' challenge to eminent domain wound its way up the courts, but the "small businessman" was ultimately no match for the Port Authority and the powers behind it. Shop owners were offered a scant $3,000 to move. Some did; others simply folded. Goliath had won. "If the considerable power of the Port Authority is allowed to dispossess the merchants of Radio Row," WCBS's Sam Slate cautioned in October 1962, "no home or business is safe from the caprice of government."

By the end of 1967, no trace of Radio Row remained.

Demolition began in the summer of 1966. "The Ajax Wrecking Company of Long Island City moved in its equipment today and began demolition of some of the first of 26 vacant buildings in Lower Manhattan," WCBS Channel 2 reporter Tom Dunn announced. "The construction of the $350 million World Trade Center may have taken another significant step." On May 2, 1967, Nadel finally threw in the towel. He wept as he watched movers clean out what was left of his inventory at 63 Cortlandt. Within a year, the entire 13-block, 16-acre site had been reduced to rubble to make way for the biggest construction project in the world. More than a million cubic yards of debris from the excavation were carted underneath the elevated West Side Highway and dumped into the Hudson River, landfill on which Battery Park City would later rise.

WITHIN A YEAR, THE ENTIRE 13-BLOCK, 16-ACRE SITE HAD BEEN REDUCED TO RUBBLE.

19 64

1822-2005

*"No one ever said cleaning up the
Fulton Fish Market was going to be easy."*

—RANDY MASTRO, MAYOR GIULIANI'S CHIEF OF STAFF, 1995

"MY FELLOW FISHERMEN AND MY FELLOW NEW YORKERS," Attorney General Robert F. Kennedy said as he greeted the buoyant mob of workers at the Fulton Fish Market at dawn on the first Wednesday of September 1964. "I have eight children, and we eat fish every Friday. From now on, we'll eat fish twice a week," he promised. "That's what we're going to do for the fishing industry of New York!" It was the first official whistle-stop of the young politician's Senate campaign. "Hundreds of fishmongers turned from their boxes of cod and mackerel," reporter R. W. Apple Jr. wrote in *The New York Times*, "to call out to Mr. Kennedy, shake his hand or wish him luck."

FULTON FISH MARKET

Clockwise from left: Dock stevedore with lobster claws, dockworker smoking a cigar, mussels merchants, all from 1943; fish handlers, 1935.

THE FULTON FISH MARKET debuted in 1822 across from the thriving South Street Seaport, which would soon be the busiest port in the world. By 1926, 394 million pounds of fish passed through Fulton annually—a quarter of all the seafood in the United States—making it the busiest fish market in the world. It inhabited a hodgepodge of structures over its 183-year history, most of which suffered major fires or other calamities, accidental and otherwise. The "Tin Building," built in 1907, narrowly survived a devastating arson fire in 1995. An annex was added in 1910, but after just 26 years its pilings buckled, sending the building's façade crumbling into the East River. The New Market Building was inaugurated by Mayor Fiorello La Guardia in 1939. Despite a few observers noting an Art Deco influence, it most closely resembled an airplane hangar. "Some people have an idea that a fish market must necessarily be unclean, unpleasant, and unsightly," La Guardia told the crowd at the ribbon cutting. "That is not true today."

The market annex lasted only 26 years, until its pilings buckled, sending the building crumbling into the East River in 1936.

KLE

BOOTH FISHERIES

BY 1926,
FULTON WAS THE BUSIEST FISH MARKET IN THE WORLD.

AS FAR BACK AS THE EARLY 1930s, NEWSPAPER HEADLINES HAD BLAZONED THE LEGAL WOES OF THE MARKET'S BAD GUYS.

Robert Kennedy's visit wasn't the first time a prominent lawman had descended on the market, and it wouldn't be the last. As far back as the early 1930s, newspaper headlines had blazoned the legal woes of the market's bad guys. In February 1982, Genovese-crime-family associate Carmine Romano, described by prosecutors as "the latest in a parade of racketeers who have ruled the industry for at least half a century," was sentenced to 12 years in prison. Just days before the 1995 Tin Building fire, Mayor Rudy Giuliani's administration had moved to seize control of the market to root out corruption. "New York City officials suspect the arson was a vivid signal from entrenched mobsters to abandon the effort," reported the *Times*. "No one ever said cleaning up the Fulton Fish Market was going to be easy," quipped Randy Mastro, Giuliani's chief of staff.

In 2005, the Fulton Fish Market departed Lower Manhattan for good, joining the old Washington Market at an industrial park in Hunts Point, the Bronx. "The creeping conversion of Manhattan into a monstrous mall for the affluent played a role," observed Dan Barry in the *Times*, "as did the grudging realization that the market had become impractical, anachronistic."

SPORTS ★★★ FINAL

THE SECRET LIFE OF TYSON'S GIRLFRIEND
EXCLUSIVE REPORT – PAGE 7

COMING FREE SUNDAY SIX FLAGS TICKETS SEE PAGE 4

DAILY NEWS
NEW YORK'S HOMETOWN NEWSPAPER

Thursday, March 30, 1995

SOMETHING FISHY

Massive arson probe in Fulton Fish Market blaze

ES, FRIDAY, AUGUST 14, 1981   L   B3

8 Indicted in Fulton Fish Market Payoffs

By ARNOLD H. LUBASCH

A union leader, two former union officials and five businessmen were indicted in Manhattan yesterday on Federal charges of racketeering, extortion and labor payoffs in the Fulton Fish Market.

Federal prosecutors also disclosed that 10 wholesale fish companies had pleaded guilty to making illegal labor payoffs to union officials. The union is Local 359 of the United Seafood Workers Union, which

"renting" union signs to 46 wholesale fish companies in the market. The signs stated that the companies employed members of Local 359.

Five businessmen were charged with collecting illegal payoffs from fish companies for officials of the union. The businessmen are John Billera, 46, of Jericho, L.I.; John Ciccarone, 64, of New Rochelle, N.Y.; Rosario Gangi, 42, of Queens; Frank Rozzo 66 of

and business interests in the fish market.

The 10 companies that have pleaded guilty to making labor payoffs could each be fined $10,000. They are the Berman Fish Company, the Blue Ribbon Fish Company, Booth Fisheries, Caleb Haley & Company, the Commercial Fish Company, R. J. Cornelius Inc., the Finest Fillet

---

THE NEW YORK TIMES, SUNDAY,

U.S. Prosecutors Say Mob Controls Fulton Market

By ARNOLD H. LUBASCH

Organized crime controls the Fulton Fish Market completely, from the arrival to the departure of the fish, according to Federal prosecutors conducting a continuing investigation.

The prosecutors, Daniel H. Bookin and Andrew J. Levander, made the accusation in a court document describing crime in the wholesale fish market, which occupies several blocks on the Lower East Side of Manhattan.

"Each year," they said, "some three-quarters of a billion dollars worth of fish passes through the market to be distributed to consumers in New York, New

Jersey, Connecticut and other parts of the Eastern United States."

"Organized crime controls every facet of the Fulton Fish Market with virtual impunity," they said. "The tribute exacted by these gangsters, moreover, is invariably passed on to New York's consumers in the form of higher food prices."

In the 38-page document, submitted for the sentencing of Carmine and Peter Romano, the prosecutors said the Romano brothers "effectively ran the Fulton Fish Market for the Genovese crime family" through their control of a seafood union.

Carmine Romano was sentenced to 12 years and his twin brother to 18 months on Federal racketeering charges involving labor payoffs in the market. Judge Lee P. Gagliardi, who sentenced them on Feb. 5, ruled last week that Carmine Romano must remain in prison pending his appeal, because he was "a danger to the community."

In their memorandum to the judge, Mr. Bookin and Mr. Levander portrayed Carmine Romano as "the boss" of the market. They said his brother, who remains free on bail, was "less powerful."

"The Genovese crime family shares some of its power in the Fulton Fish

Market with[ly," the p]
scribed in a
latest in a
have ruled
a century."

Le
"The Fu
by Local 35
ers Union,
who handl
continued.
ers Union,
by organiz
"As far
was dom
Lanza, a
family."
Local
power" o

MONUMENTAL DEMOLITION

"WE WILL PROBABLY BE JUDGED NOT BY THE MONUMENTS WE BUILD," WROTE ADA LOUISE HUXTABLE IN OCTOBER 1963, AS DEMOLITION OF THE ORIGINAL PENN STATION BEGAN, "BUT BY THOSE WE HAVE DESTROYED." JUST AS THE TWIN TOWERS WERE STARTING TO RISE FOUR YEARS LATER, THE 612-FOOT-TALL SINGER BUILDING—ONCE THE TALLEST IN THE WORLD—WAS BEING DISMANTLED BRICK BY BRICK, COLUMN BY COLUMN, A FEW BLOCKS AWAY AT LIBERTY AND BROADWAY. IT WAS THE TALLEST BUILDING EVER VOLUNTARILY RAZED, A TITLE IT HELD UNTIL THE DEMOLITION OF J. P. MORGAN CHASE'S 707-FOOT-TALL 270 PARK AVENUE HEADQUARTERS, WHICH BEGAN IN 2019.

When the Beaux-Arts-style Singer Building opened in 1908, it was the tallest office tower in the world. Visitors paid 50 cents for a ride up to the 40th-floor observation deck.

1967

United States Steel bought the Singer Building in 1964. Demolition began in 1967 and was completed the following year. In its place would rise the company's new Skidmore, Owings & Merrill–designed, 54-story International Style headquarters.

TWIN TOWERS: CITIES IN THE SKY

1964 — 2001

68

TWIN TOWER SPECS

Height, north tower:
1,368 feet

Height, south tower:
1,362 feet

Floors, each tower: 110

Total Square Feet: 10 million

Opened: 1972

Cost: $900 million

Architect:
Minoru Yamasaki

Associate architects:
Emery Roth & Sons

Developer:
The Port Authority

Construction manager:
Tishman Realty & Construction

Occupancy: 50,000

Exclusive Zip Code: 10048

"**THE TOWERS ARE PURE TECHNOLOGY,** the lobbies are pure schmaltz," wrote Ada Louise Huxtable in her characteristically unsparing review of the new World Trade Center on April 5, 1973. "The Port Authority has built the ultimate Disneyland fairytale blockbuster." And a block buster it was: 13 vibrant city blocks pulverized to make way for not just the tallest building in the world but two of them. Huxtable wasn't alone in her skepticism. Among other slights directed at the towers: "glass and metal filing cabinets," "a pair of middle fingers," "arrogant twins," "the boxes the Empire State and Chrysler buildings came in," and "the largest aluminum siding job in the history of the world."

STARTING OCT. 26 THE NEW YORK SKYLINE WILL NEVER BE THE SAME.

SESAME STREET

Monsters on the Loose!

October, 1976 60¢

Harrison Ford   Sigourney Weaver

Melanie Griffith

The closest some of us will ever get to heaven.

THE WORLD TRADE CENTER NEW YORK

DESPITE THE HARSH RECEPTION, the Twin Towers were a marvel of design and engineering innovation in their day. Think tube frames, sky lobbies, viscoelastic dampers, spandrel plates. Twelve thousand miles of electrical cable carried more than a half-million kilowatt-hours of electricity daily, enough to power a medium-size city. Eventually more than 20,000 workers would ride each tower's 99 passenger elevators to 110 acre-size office floors. Among the major tenants were Morgan Stanley, Aon, Cantor Fitzgerald, and Marsh & McClennan. In all, more than 430 companies from 28 countries. By the time they were teenagers, the Twin Towers were iconic symbols of global capitalism, featured on postcards, in Hollywood movies, on TV shows, and in advertising campaigns.

DESIGN

IN 1962, THE WORLD'S FAIR would again factor in the evolution of the World Trade Center. Instead of Flushing Meadows, Queens, this time the setting was downtown Seattle. President Kennedy had just vowed to put a man on the moon before the decade's end, and the theme of the fair was "The Age of Space." A 32-year-old World War II veteran and civil servant from New York named Guy Tozzoli had been wandering the grounds. Other than the 605-foot-tall Space Needle, little had impressed him. But when he came upon the Century 21 Exposition's Science Pavilion, "something froze him in place,"

THE TWIN TOWERS WERE A MARVEL OF DESIGN AND ENGINEERING INNOVATION IN THEIR DAY.

James Glanz and Eric Lipton wrote in *City in the Sky*. "Here amid an orgy of noise was a marvelously cool and inviting palace, a constructed space with the serenity of a natural sanctuary."

Tozzoli wasn't just any tourist. He'd recently been assigned by Port Authority executive director Austin J. Tobin to oversee all aspects of the new World Trade Center project. Tozzoli had never heard the name Minoru Yamasaki, but within a few months he'd convinced his bosses to hire the 49-year-old, Detroit-based architect behind the Science Pavilion. Never mind that the unassuming Yamasaki had little else in his portfolio besides a handful of airport terminals and a St. Louis housing project. Or that he'd never designed a building taller than 32 stories and nothing at all in New York City. "Over the next fifteen years," wrote Glanz and Lipton, "these two oddly matched men would become friends and bitter rivals, confidants and enemies, colleagues and competitors."

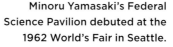

Minoru Yamasaki's Federal Science Pavilion debuted at the 1962 World's Fair in Seattle.

Yamasaki struggled with the sheer scale of the commission: 10 million square feet. But Tozzoli insisted on "catalytic bigness," a term David Rockefeller had coined, meaning something so big it couldn't be ignored, so overwhelming it would spawn additional development. When "Yama," as Tozzoli had taken to calling him, presented a plan featuring a scant eight million square feet—two million short—Tozzoli didn't mince words. "Yama, President Kennedy is going to put a man on the moon, and you're going to figure out a way to build me the tallest buildings in the world." Despite the added cost, Tobin and Tozzoli had calculated that the marketing upside to building the tallest office towers in the history of humanity was priceless, even if, as Yamasaki pointed out, the title would almost certainly be temporary.

Inspired by his idol Ludwig Mies van der Rohe's identical Lake Shore Drive apartment towers in Chicago and Venice's Piazza San Marco, and borrowing motifs such

Clockwise from left: Guy Tozzoli, director of the Port Authority's World Trade Department, 1962; architect Minoru Yamasaki, 1960; Yamasaki and his team with a model of the World Trade Center, 1967.

Architect Minoru Yamasaki and Governor Nelson Rockefeller view a model of the World Trade Center, January 16, 1964.

as the Gothic arches from his own Seattle Science Pavilion and the slender vertical windows from his Michigan Consolidated Gas Company Building in Detroit, Yamasaki unveiled his revamped World Trade Center design on January 18, 1964. "My God, these towers will make David's building look like an outhouse," Governor Nelson Rockefeller—referring to One Chase Manhattan Plaza—remarked after inspecting Yamasaki's model.

Even before ground was broken, Yamasaki's towers were pummeled by critics. "These incredible giants just stand there, artless and dumb," wrote Wolf Von Eckardt in the May 1966 issue of *Harper's*, "without any relationship to anything, not even to each other." *The Nation* dubbed them "Manhattan's Tower of Babel" and *New York* magazine declared the towers "a striking example of socialism at its worst." Ada Louise Huxtable was only slightly more forgiving, wondering if they would be "the start of a new skyscraper age or the biggest tombstones in the world."

"THESE TOWERS WILL MAKE DAVID'S BUILDING LOOK LIKE AN OUTHOUSE."

Workers lower the first 34-ton grillage into the pit, August 6, 1968.

CONSTRUCTION

THE PORT AUTHORITY had confidence in Yamasaki's design but admitted it would require "engineering ingenuity from foundation to roof." The first order of business: figure out how to keep the Hudson River out of the basement. The solution was "the bathtub"—a 70-foot-deep, three-foot-thick, 3,294-foot-long reinforced-concrete slurry wall—in which the two towers would stand. Holding the parallelogram-shaped bathtub's walls upright would be more than a thousand steel cables, called tiebacks, drilled into the surrounding bedrock. More than a million cubic yards of earth had to be excavated, most of it hauled underneath the West Side Elevated Highway and dumped into the Hudson River, landfill on which Battery Park City would later rise. Among the artifacts found during excavation were clay pipes, cannonballs, ships' anchors, and British coins pre-dating the American Revolution.

THE FIRST ORDER OF BUSINESS:
KEEP THE HUDSON RIVER OUT OF THE BASEMENT.

On August 8, 1968, Richard Nixon accepted his party's nomination for president at the Republican National Convention in Miami, soundly defeating Governor Nelson Rockefeller, who, along with his younger brother David, had willed the World Trade Center from an underwhelming exhibit at the 1939 World's Fair into the largest urban-renewal project in the nation's history. Two days earlier, workers had carefully lowered the first steel grillage into the bathtub, the first piece of what Glanz and Lipton called "the biggest and most complicated jigsaw

puzzle in the world." In all, 192,000 tons of structural steel would be raised, much of it in the form of pre-fabricated panels, an innovation that helped dramatically speed up the pace of construction. Another remarkable innovation was the use of viscoelastic dampers, or "shock absorbers," to mitigate the oscillation of the towers in high winds, without which, engineers worried, inhabitants of the upper floors would be plagued by motion sickness. Eleven thousand of the dampers were installed in each tower.

Two days before Christmas 1970, the north tower was topped out. A cloud-shrouded ceremony at 1,368 feet marked the milestone. Construction workers and V.I.P.'s, including Tozzoli and Tobin, strained to watch the final column as it was raised by crane through the cool, damp air to the roof, followed by a 30-foot-tall Christmas tree. Seven months later the scene was played out again, minus the Christmas tree, atop the south tower.

World Trade Center construction worker, 1970.

In all, more than 10,000 construction workers were enlisted to build the Twin Towers—roughly 3,600 on any given day—from dozens of trades and unions, installing 2.2 million square feet of aluminum siding, 43,600 windows, 40,000 doors, 170 miles of pipe, 7,000 plumbing fixtures, 23,000 fluorescent lights, and 6,500 sensors feeding data to computers regulating air-conditioning and heating. Not to mention 425,000 cubic yards of concrete, enough "to build a sidewalk from New York City to Washington, D.C.," according to the 9/11 Memorial. Only nine workers died in the construction of the towers, reported *The New York Times*, a remarkable safety record for a project of such scale at the time.

A CLOUD-SHROUDED CEREMONY AT 1,368 FEET
MARKED THE MILESTONE.

DEDICATION

THE OFFICIAL DEDICATION CEREMONY had been scheduled to take place on the plaza between the two towers on Wednesday morning, April 4, 1973. But as is often the case downtown, where the mighty Hudson River meets the Atlantic tide, rain and gusty winds buffeted the plaza and towers above, forcing organizers to move the event into the lobby of the north tower. A statement was read from President Nixon, who predicted the World Trade Center would be "a major factor for the expansion of the nation's international trade." New Jersey governor William Cahill promised it would "promote harmony and commerce" between New York and New Jersey. Governor Nelson Rockefeller called the towers "a great marriage of utility and beauty."

Conspicuously absent were three V.I.P.'s. Secretary of Labor Peter Brennan, who was to have read Nixon's address, refused to cross a picket line of striking PATH workers and left. Mayor John Lindsay, who had repeatedly clashed with the Port Authority over the Trade Center, was a no-show. Not even Austin Tobin, who had recently retired after 30 years running the Port Authority, bothered to attend. When asked the next day why he'd been absent, Tobin replied, "It was raining."

World Trade Center dedication ceremony, April 4, 1973.

Ada Louise Huxtable's views didn't thaw much after touring the towers and their "pure schmaltz" lobbies. Citing the narrow, 22-inch-wide windows, "one of the miraculous benefits of the tall building, the panoramic view out, is destroyed," she wrote in her *Times* review of the towers. "No amount of head-dodging from column to column can put that fragmented view together. It is pure visual frustration."

In response to critics, Yamasaki released a statement defending his architectural proclivities. "As regards the narrow windows," he wrote, "they give me none, if any, sense of acrophobia." He quoted Ralph Waldo Emerson ("Beauty rests on necessities") and begrudged the proliferation of all-glass buildings. "As for mirror glass, I detest it, because buildings with it look to me as if they have cataracts, showing

no life within," he wrote. Yamasaki also highlighted a few of the immense engineering challenges that were overcome to build the Twin Towers, then offered up a characteristically humble summation: "I am not implying by this statement that these buildings are great. That is perhaps not for any of us to say now, but for the people to decide in the many years during which the buildings will live."

19
73

"If you try to use the West Side Highway in the next three months, you'll regret it."
— Mayor John Lindsay, September 1973

THE END OF MILLER HIGHWAY

MORNING RUSH HOUR, DECEMBER 15, 1973.

Fifty-one-year-old truck driver Nicholas Perrone, working for the Queens-based Edenwald Contracting Company, was inching his way south on the West Side Highway carrying a load of asphalt to a crew patching up the road's pockmarked southbound lanes. As Perrone approached Little West 12th Street, the highway began to shimmy—then buckle—beneath him. He leapt from the truck's cab just as it rolled over and tumbled 40 feet down to West Street below, taking a tailing four-door Lincoln sedan with it. Perrone was rescued by an F.D.N.Y. ladder company as he dangled from the precipice of the broken highway. Incredibly he suffered only minor injuries, as did the driver of the sedan, which landed on a heap of crumbled pavement and twisted rebar a few yards from the truck.

The West Side Highway, August 15, 1973, precisely four months before the collapse.

"IN A THUNDEROUS RAIN OF GRANITE AND STEEL, [the] big tractor-trailer plunged into West St. below, miraculously crashing down atop nobody," the *Daily News* reported. "Hours later the luckless drivers trapped between Canal and Gansevoort still were tortuously inching backward, trying to get off the West Side Highway that all at once wasn't there anymore." Within 48 hours, officials had announced the "indefinite closure" of the highway below 18th Street.

Built in sections between 1927 and 1951, it was named after Manhattan borough president Julius Miller, but would soon be known simply as the West Side Highway. At its inception, it was considered a remarkable urban-design innovation, the city's—arguably the world's—first elevated expressway. By 1936, it ran from the Battery all the way up to West 72nd Street, where it merged with the Henry Hudson Parkway. Robert Moses promised New Yorkers that this "gleaming new concrete ribbon" and "veritable motorist's dream," as the press praised it, would shave a whopping 42 minutes off the drive from Canal Street to the Yonkers city line. "Once upon a time an engineering marvel," as the *Daily News* would later note, the West Side Highway declined into a chronically snarled "teeth-rattling old elevated washboard." By the early 1970s, it had become a symbol of urban-infrastructure blight, along with the city's subway system, which at the time had fallen into such disrepair that less than two-thirds of its trains reached their destinations on time (a statistic embarrassingly revisited again in 2017).

Perrone's truck tumbled 40 feet down to West Street.

MILLER HIGHWAY, AT ITS INCEPTION, WAS CONSIDERED A REMARKABLE URBAN-DESIGN INNOVATION.

Engineers determined the highway's collapse had been caused by the "severe deterioration" of its steel supporting beams. No surprise, given the roadbed's penchant for collecting rainwater, often six inches deep and infused with corrosive rock salt in the wintertime. It didn't help when investigators determined that Edenwald's truck had been ladened with 30 tons of asphalt, nine tons over the legal limit. (Apparently it didn't hurt either, as Edenwald was reportedly awarded a no-bid contract to clean up the wreckage.)

As the highway was gradually dismantled between 1977 and 1989—in increments, just as it had been erected—its remaining spans became elevated concrete playgrounds. Adventurous urbanites trespassed the on-ramps up to the perilous roadbed in order to take in the dystopian vistas, two decades before the High Line would make re-purposing dilapidated infrastructure trendy.

"ONCE UPON A TIME AN ENGINEERING MARVEL," IT WOULD DECLINE INTO A CHRONICALLY SNARLED "TEETH-RATTLING OLD ELEVATED WASHBOARD."

A section of the
West Side Highway
at Canal Street in
January 1981, almost
a decade after it
was condemned.

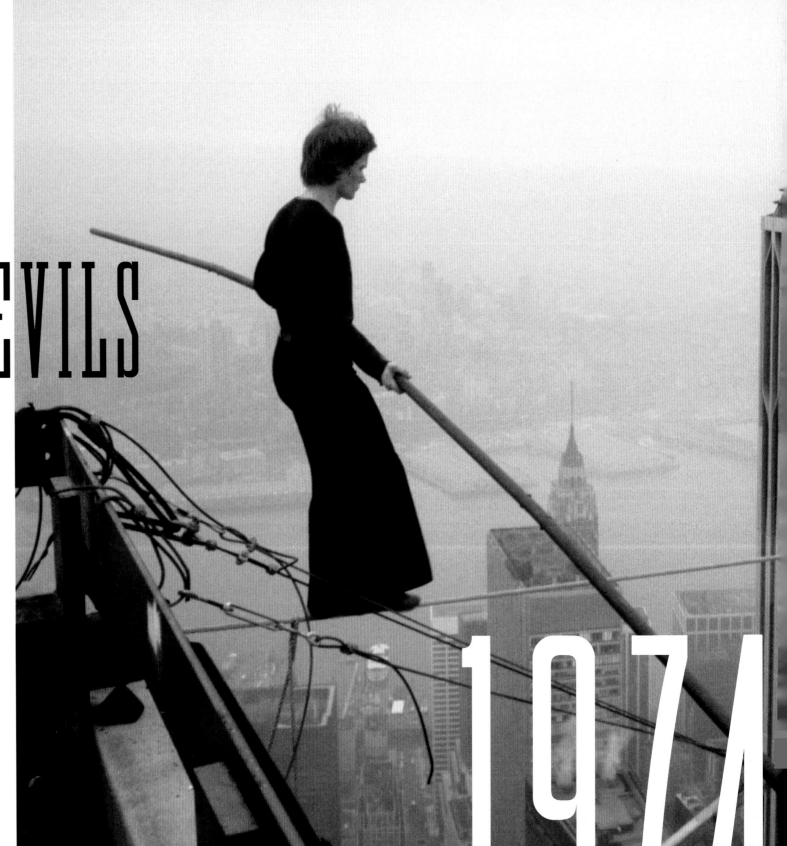

THE
DAREDEVILS

1974

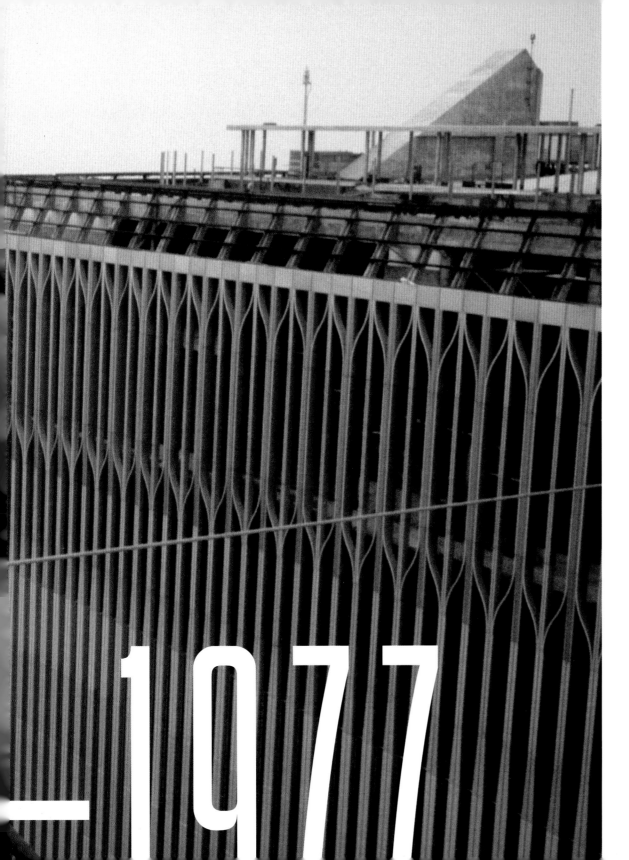

1977

MAN ON WIRE

August 7, 1974

"THERE IS NO WHY."

—PHILIPPE PETIT

"I AM A JUGGLER AND A HIGH-WIRE WALKER," Philippe Petit, handcuffed to a metal chair in the First Precinct, replied when asked by a reporter why he did it. "When I see three oranges I must juggle them. When I see two beautiful towers I must walk between them." When asked how he did it: "By a long, long preparation." Petit spent five months readying himself for the stunt and was the first daredevil to conquer the Twin Towers—and the hearts of the tens of thousands of New Yorkers who watched him do it. The reward was immeasurable. "After all the work, the day comes," he marveled, "and it's the most beautiful day of your life."

"YOU FEEL LIKE YOU'RE THE KING OF THE WORLD, THE KING OF THE SKY."

Presenting fake IDs, Petit and his accomplices had made their way to the top of each tower, posing as contractors. Under cover of darkness, using a bow and arrow, they managed to rig up the 450-pound, 200-foot steel cable Petit would use for his walk between the towers, a quarter mile above the plaza. Just after seven A.M., wearing all black, Petit set out on the wire. Within half an hour, tens of thousands of New Yorkers had gathered to watch, heads craned skyward, as Petit walked, danced, lied down for an apparent "nap," and saluted them. By the next morning, he was an international sensation. *The New York Times* praised him for combining "the cunning of a second-story man with the nerve of an Evel Knievel."

"The police took a humorless view of the act," noted NBC News correspondent Robert Hager, and arrested Petit for trespassing and disorderly conduct. But by early afternoon, the charges had been dropped, after Petit agreed to give a free aerial performance in Central Park for schoolchildren (a sentence he later called "the most beautiful punishment I could have received"). Credited with bringing a much-needed P.R. boost to a new World Trade Center struggling to find tenants, Petit was rewarded with a lifetime pass to the south tower's observation deck. "It's magnificent the way he did it," an incredulous N.Y.P.D. officer told Hager. Petit himself was incredulous: "I still don't believe I did it. I must now look at pictures and movies to be sure I did."

THE QUEENS SKYDIVER

July 22, 1975

"WITH MEN THIS IS IMPOSSIBLE, BUT WITH GOD ALL THINGS ARE POSSIBLE."

—MATTHEW 19:26

JUST BEFORE THE END OF BUSINESS on July 22, 1975, New York State Department of Social Services employee Gerry Lewinter was getting ready to leave his office on the 29th floor of the south tower when he saw "a white blur outside and looked up to see a parachute going down." The white blur was 34-year-old father of three Owen J. Quinn, who'd posed as a construction worker to get to the roof of the north tower and, wearing a silver helmet and a football jersey inscribed with the biblical verse Matthew 19:26, hurled himself off the building. He free-fell 600 feet while his chute "hesitated" before opening, then a gust of wind blew him into the side of the building, injuring his leg. The descent took less than two minutes. "He seemed to hit very hard," Lewinter told *The New York Times*. "He got up and started walking, limping for about 25 steps. Then he sat down. He seemed to be in pain."

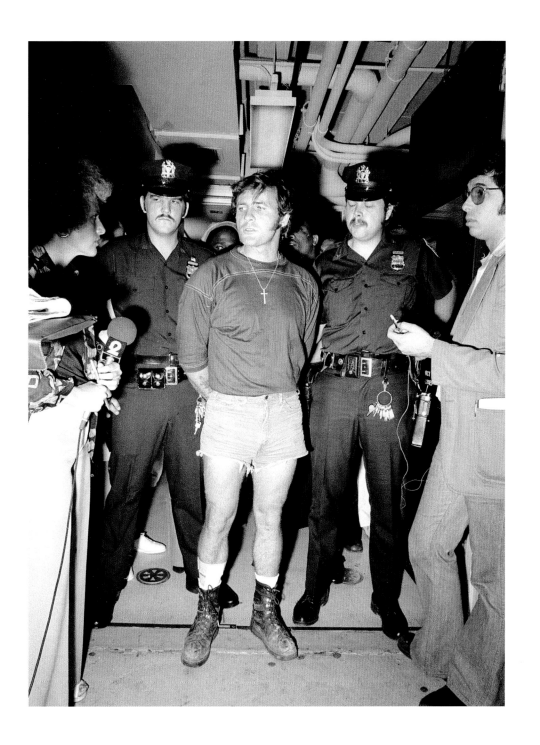

AFTER BEING DECLARED OFFICIALLY SANE, QUINN WAS CHARGED WITH CRIMINAL TRESPASS AND RECKLESS ENDANGERMENT.

Quinn was taken to Beekman Downtown Hospital for X-rays then to Elmhurst General Hospital in Queens for psychiatric evaluation. After being declared officially sane, he was charged with criminal trespass and reckless endangerment. When asked what motivated his jump, he said he wanted to draw attention to the plight of the poor. "If people decided not to eat once a month and to send the money to the needy poor," he told the *Times*, "then it would help the situation."

THE HUMAN FLY

May 26, 1977

"JUST ANOTHER CLIMB."

—GEORGE WILLIG

IT WAS 6:30 A.M., MAY 26, 1977, and 27-year-old Queens-based toy designer and amateur mountaineer George Willig had just begun his ascent up the south tower, using homemade clamps he'd fashioned for the building's vertical window-washing grooves. His first moves were stealthy ones. By the time police arrived, he was already well beyond reach. "The only way out of here is up," he thought to himself as he continued skyward.

Cops inflated a 20-by-35-foot airbag in case Willig slipped, then descended in a window-washing basket and met him at the 55th floor. Two officers tried to coax him in. He politely declined but signed an autograph for them. ("Best wishes to my co-ascenders," it read.) Later, he stopped for a snack at the 70th floor (a cinnamon bun with honey) while no fewer than six helicopters hovered nearby, broadcasting his remarkable stunt to a rapt, proliferating morning-news audience.

When he reached the top floor, he crawled through a small roof hatch and was promptly arrested for criminal trespass, reckless endangerment, and disorderly conduct. A swarm of reporters later cornered him outside the First Precinct. "Why did you do it?" one asked. "Just another climb," Willig replied. Another reporter prodded: "Is there a lesson you can tell people that you've learned?" Willig: "Well, I don't think anybody else should do it." The city announced its intention to slap Willig with a $250,000 lawsuit to cover police overtime. But after public outcry, the penalty was reduced to $1.10, a penny for each of the 110 stories he'd scaled. "Demonstrations of this spirit are sometimes rewarded with medals, honors, knighthoods," *NBC Nightly News* anchor John Chancellor told viewers that evening, "and in some cases, citations for disorderly conduct." The *Daily News* later declared it "an epic ascent that would transfix and thrill a crime-battered, debt-ridden metropolis badly in need of a distraction."

"THE ONLY WAY OUT OF HERE IS UP," WILLIG THOUGHT TO HIMSELF.

LANDFILL CITY:
RIVIERA ON THE HUDSON

"TWO ACRES OF NORTH DAKOTA WHEAT, just turned amber, wave in the sea breeze on the Battery Park City landfill," reported *The New York Times* on August 2, 1982. "To look across this wheat field is to see the Statue of Liberty, Ellis Island and boat traffic as in a surreal illusion." These urban waves of grain were the creation of SoHo conceptual artist Agnes Denes, who called it "an intrusion of the country into the metropolis, the world's richest real estate." After "lunch hour visits in three-piece suits," she told the *Times*, it drew "a praying mantis and fireflies."

19

82

A

ACCORDING TO PORT AUTHORITY

chief Austin Tobin, Battery Park City was the brainchild of his World Trade Center deputy, Guy Tozzoli, who'd dreamt it up while shaving one morning in 1966. Why not just deposit all that dirt and rubble from the World Trade Center excavation—more than a million cubic yards of it—into the Hudson River to make more Manhattan? Governor Nelson Rockefeller agreed and took it up a notch, proposing a 98-acre, S600 million mixed-use

WHY NOT JUST DEPOSIT ALL THAT RUBBLE FROM THE EXCAVATION INTO THE HUDSON TO MAKE MORE MANHATTAN?

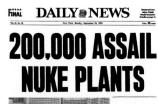

Nearly 200,000 people gathered on Battery Park City's landfill on September 23, 1979, to protest against the nation's use of nuclear energy. "The protesters were met by a cloudless blue sky," reported *The New York Times,* "while the sun—the alternative energy source they promoted—glistened off the World Trade Center towers looming nearby."

development—"a Riviera on the Hudson," as critics derided it, citing other parts of the city in desperate need of renewal.

In May 1973, a month after their dedication ceremony, the Twin Towers lost the title of tallest buildings in the world—to the Sears Tower in Chicago—as Minoru Yamasaki had predicted. Across the street, where more than a dozen bustling piers had once loaded and unloaded passengers and freight from all over the world, the vacant landfill came to be known as "the Beach," for its "dunes" made of sand dredged from Lower New York Bay's Ambrose Channel. By decade's end, no construction had yet begun. Local officials had had bigger fish to fry: the city was hemorrhaging hundreds of thousands of jobs and only narrowly averted bankruptcy in 1975. Its infrastructure was crumbling, and crime was rampant. "After a decade of planners' dreams and bureaucrats' schemes," wrote Joseph P. Fried in *The*

The $1.5 billion, seven-million-square-foot World Financial Center opened on October 17, 1985. Its anchor tenants included Merrill Lynch, American Express, and Dow Jones, earning it *The New York Times* headline: FINALLY, THE DEBUT OF WALL STREET WEST.

"IT WAS A PROMISING FRONTIER."

New York Times, "the attempt to build a 'new town' along the Hudson River waterfront in Lower Manhattan is still surrounded by uncertainty."

Battery Park City's first residential towers, the 1,712-unit Gateway Plaza, didn't open until 1982, just as Agnes Denes was planting her wheat field a half-mile to the south. Author and journalist Glenn Plaskin moved into Gateway a few years later, in July 1985. "It was a promising frontier, a little like the Wild West," he recalls. "There was just one of everything: one dry cleaner, one grocery store, one liquor store, one bank, one drugstore. It was a one-of-a-kind neighborhood to be sure." But the low rents and spectacular views had enticed Plaskin. "People walked into my living room and their eyes went directly to the river," he remembers, "sailboats and yachts coming and going, the coast of New Jersey still undeveloped." Battery Park City slowly grew from its original 23 acres to 92, and by 2018 its residential population had reached 16,000 while Lower Manhattan's topped 60,000.

"Denes planted six bushels and estimated the harvest at 40," wrote Henry Mitchell in *The Washington Post* on August 18, 1982, "not quite up to the biblical hundred-fold, but then this is a naughty world." In the background, tenants had just started moving into Battery Park City's first residential apartment complex, Gateway Plaza.

BASEMENT BOMBING

AROUND NOON ON FEBRUARY 26, 1993, A 24-YEAR-OLD KUWAITI NAMED RAMZI YOUSEF AND AN ACCOMPLICE PARKED A YELLOW FORD ECONOLINE RENTAL VAN ON THE B-2 LEVEL OF THE PUBLIC GARAGE BENEATH THE TWIN TOWERS. A FEW MINUTES LATER, A 1,500-POUND COCKTAIL OF UREA NITRATE AND OTHER EXPLOSIVES DETONATED, RIPPING A 150-FOOT-WIDE, FIVE-STORY-DEEP CRATER AND KILLING SIX PEOPLE INSTANTLY. SUCH WAS THE FORCE OF THE BLAST THAT IT WAS FELT ON THE TOP FLOORS OF BOTH TOWERS. IT ALSO KNOCKED OUT ALL ELECTRICAL POWER, TRAPPING HUNDREDS OF PEOPLE IN DOZENS OF ELEVATORS. TENS OF THOUSANDS MORE STRUGGLED TO DESCEND SMOKE-FILLED, PITCH-BLACK STAIRWELLS. IT WAS NEARLY 12 HOURS BEFORE EVERYONE WAS EVACUATED.

1993

Within hours of the blast, Yousef was on a flight to Pakistan. He had hoped that the force of the bomb would send the north tower crashing into the south tower. Yousef's uncle, Khalid Sheikh Mohammed, had helped finance the plot and would go on to mastermind the 9/11 attacks eight years later.

$2,000,000
REWARD

At approximately 12 noon on February 26, 1993, a massive explosion rocked the World Trade Center in New York City, causing millions of dollars in damage. The terrorists who bombed the World Trade Center murdered six innocent people, injured over 1,000 others, and left terrified school children trapped for hours in smoke filled elevators.

Following the bombing, law enforcement officials obtained evidence which led to the indictments and arrests of several suspected terrorists involved in the bombing. RAMZI AHMED YOUSEF, one of those indicted, fled the United States immediately after the bombing to avoid arrest. YOUSEF is now a fugitive from justice. YOUSEF was born in Iraq or Kuwait, possesses Iraqi and Pakistani passports, and also claims to be a citizen of the United Arab Emirates. Because of the nature of the crimes for which he is charged, YOUSEF should be considered armed and extremely dangerous.

The United States Department of State is offering a reward of up to $2,000,000 for information leading to the apprehension and prosecution of YOUSEF. If you have information about YOUSEF or the World Trade Center bombing, contact the authorities, or the nearest U.S. embassy or consulate. In the United States, call your local office of the Federal Bureau of Investigation or 1-800-HEROES1, or write to:

HEROES
Post Office Box 96781
Washington, D.C. 20090 - 6781
U.S.A.

RAMZI AHMED YOUSEF
DESCRIPTION

DATE OF BIRTH: May 20, 1967 and/or April 27, 1968
PLACE OF BIRTH: Iraq, Kuwait, or United Arab Emirates
HEIGHT: 5'
WEIGHT: 180 pounds
BUILD: medium
HAIR: brown
EYES: brown
COMPLEXION: olive
SEX: male
RACE: white
CHARACTERISTICS: sometimes is clean shaven
ALIASES: Ramzi A. Yousef, Ramzi Ahmad Yousef, Ramzi Yousef, Ramzi Yousef Ahmed, Ramzi Yousef Ahmed, Rasheed Yousef, Rashid Rashid, Rashid, Kamal Ibraham, Kamal Abraham, Abraham Kamal, Kamal Kemal, Muhammad Azan, Khurram Khan,

00

THE
BIDDING
WAR

"They had to
be cardboard,"
Silverstein remarked
of the ceremonial
keys, "or else you
couldn't lift them."

BY THE LATE 1990s, the Port Authority was facing increasing political pressure from both Albany and Trenton to privatize the, by then, iconic Twin Towers. In late 2000, the agency began soliciting bids from private developers. Soon three of the biggest names in New York real estate were facing off in an unprecedented bidding war: Steve Roth, Mort Zuckerman, and Larry Silverstein. Although Roth outbid his rivals with a $3.25 billion offer for the 99-year lease, his negotiations with the Port Authority stalled, and Silverstein, once considered the dark horse, suddenly found himself the frontrunner. "We're lusting for the World Trade Center," he told the *New York Post* on January 30, 2001, "the prize of all prizes."

2000 – 2001

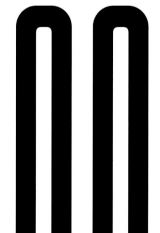

B

BORN AND RAISED IN BEDFORD-STUYVESANT, Brooklyn, Larry Silverstein followed his father into the commercial-real-estate brokerage business after graduating from New York University in 1952. Emulating mentors Harry Helmsley and Larry Wien, he cobbled together a syndicate of small investors and bought his first property in 1957, a run-down industrial loft building on East 23rd Street in Manhattan, converted it to office space, and leased it out to up-and-coming firms for a tidy profit.

Larry Silverstein signs an agreement to lease the World Trade Center, July 24, 2001.

IT WAS THE BIGGEST REAL-ESTATE TRANSACTION IN NEW YORK HISTORY.

By 1987 he had built his first skyscraper, 7 World Trade Center, on land leased from the Port Authority.

On April 26, 2001, Silverstein and the Port Authority's newly appointed executive director, Neil Levin, announced a deal: Silverstein would make a down payment of $491 million against a purchase price of $3.22 billion for the 99-year lease and agree to pay an annual ground rent of $120 million. It was the biggest real-estate transaction in New York history. The lease ran 1,160 pages.

On the morning of September 11, Silverstein had planned to have a breakfast meeting at Windows on the World, in the north tower, one of the top-grossing restaurants in the country. But Silverstein's wife, Klara, insisted he keep a dermatology appointment, and he begrudgingly complied. Neil Levin wasn't as lucky. He was on the 107th floor of the north tower having breakfast when the first plane struck, 10 floors below. He never made it out of the building.

Above from left: Roger Silverstein, Lisa Silverstein, Klara Silverstein, Larry Silverstein, and Lenny Boxer, July 24, 2001.

Left: Silverstein poses with Robert Linton—chairman of original 7 World Trade Center anchor tenant Drexel Burnham Lambert, which would later pull out of the deal—in a full-page ad, 1986.

20 01

1990 – 2001

WITNESS: THREE DAYS AT GROUND ZERO

"MY FIRST IMPRESSION OF NEW YORK was that it was a big, brash, beautiful city, full of energy and passion for creative endeavors," says photographer Joe Woolhead, who arrived in 1990 from his native Ireland. He picked up a string of "menial jobs" to make ends meet, including a busboy gig at a restaurant on a sublevel of the World Trade Center. "I worked there for one day," he recalls, chuckling, "and then they fired me." But he took the occasion to make a trip up to the observation deck of the south tower, elevation 1,377 feet. "It was a pretty mind-blowing experience to see how vast the city was from such a great height," he remembers. "You get a different sense of grandeur about it."

WOOLHEAD FIRST GOT INTO PHOTOGRAPHY at age 10
"when I picked up a camera at a wedding and took a really bad
picture." But his dad took note and gave him a little hand-me-
down Kodak Instamatic. (His brother later got him a 35-mm.
Canon AE-1.) He started taking pictures of friends, landscapes,
nature, but "it was all amateurish stuff," he says of his teenage
work. It wasn't until he discovered the photography department's
darkroom at Rathmines College in Dublin, where he was a film
student, that he really started to get the "feel" for photography.

By September 11, 2001, Woolhead had gotten a green card
and been living in New York City for more than a decade.
He'd worked dozens of construction jobs, everything from
demolition to bricklaying, suffered a terrible accident that

crushed his legs and put him out of work, prevailed in a workers'-compensation lawsuit, and started taking film classes at Hunter College. He was at home in his apartment in Jackson Heights, Queens, listening to *The Howard Stern Show*, when the news broke that a plane had hit the north tower of the World Trade Center. "I only had $10 to my name," he recalls, but he grabbed his camera, picked up 10 rolls of film at a 99-cent store in Sunnyside, and hopped on the 7 train to Manhattan.

Woolhead got off the subway at Canal Street and "immediately bolted down West Broadway" against a stampede of thousands of dazed office workers fleeing north. He got as far as

HE WAS AT HOME IN HIS APARTMENT IN QUEENS WHEN THE NEWS BROKE THAT A PLANE HAD HIT THE NORTH TOWER.

"THIS IS THE NORTH TOWER FROM WORTH STREET SHOWING THE DAMAGE SUSTAINED FROM THE PLANE'S IMPACT. WITHIN 10 MINUTES, THIS BUILDING WAS GONE."

Chambers Street when he heard a huge rumbling sound. In the time it took him to snap six shots, the second tower had fallen. "The plume of this colossal wreckage just bloomed up and was racing down the street like a freight train," he recalls. A cop standing at the entrance to a hotel motioned him to get inside. He watched from the lobby as West Broadway went pitch-black, streetlights automatically flickering on to reveal a blizzard-like scene outside. But instead of snow, a foot-deep blanket of toxic dust, office papers, and other debris covered the street. Despite reports that more planes had been hijacked, Woolhead asked a hotel maid for a wet cloth to put over his face and went out again into "the chaos."

Woolhead eventually ran into a fellow Irishman who snuck him through the police cordon ringing the site. "Come here, I want to show you something," the man told him. Woolhead followed to the edge of a smoldering crater where 6 World Trade Center had stood only hours before. There, down in the pit beneath them, was a steel cross that had "sort of pitched itself into the collapsed wreckage around it," Woolhead recalls. "I was almost in tears when I took that photograph. It brought up a lot of emotions that I was trying to dampen so I could simply work." But a police officer had spotted him with his camera, and he was escorted off the site. Woolhead was later told that 12 bodies had been found "in a heap" beneath the cross. "They were fleeing out of the building, and they didn't make it."

Determined to get back in, he approached a man in a green HAZMAT suit on West Street, who took him to a makeshift command center that had been set up in Stuyvesant High School, in Battery Park City, where he would spend the night. "People were wandering around aimlessly," he recalls of the scene inside. "I would talk to a soldier here, a worker there. And then I spoke to a doctor, and he had nothing to do. There were no survivors. There was nobody else to be pulled out. Everybody was dead. And I think even he knew it."

"The plume of this colossal wreckage just bloomed up and was racing down the street like a freight train."

The next morning, Woolhead helped unload boxes of work boots for the recovery workers, who had started streaming in from all over the region: volunteer firefighters, ironworkers, welders, general contractors, truck drivers. Supplies were pouring into the command center: "Toothbrushes, toothpaste, cups, everything, it was all being piled up inside." That afternoon, Woolhead snuck back onto the site by shadowing a team of F.B.I. agents through a checkpoint and took dozens more photographs. Worried he might be stopped and his film confiscated, he hid the spent rolls underneath his hard hat. "I was wandering around with all this film rattling around on my head," he recalls, "and trying not to be noticed by anyone."

Eventually Woolhead was approached by a suspicious N.Y.P.D. officer. "He called over his commanding officer, and then the commanding officer called over a soldier, and the soldier called over a major. When the major saw me, he was looking at me and listening to my excuse that I had sort of wandered away from where I'd been working at Ground Zero—a complete fabrication—and he just told me, 'Look, go fuck off.' And I said, 'O.K.,' and I went because I was glad they didn't even check my bag." He doubled back by the waterfront and watched as a frantic crowd of Battery Park City residents, whom the authorities had given an hour to collect personal belongings, "charged, literally ran back into their apartments to gather their stuff."

"I WAS ALMOST IN TEARS WHEN I TOOK THIS PHOTOGRAPH, BECAUSE I COULDN'T BELIEVE HOW THIS CROSS OF STEEL HAD PITCHED ITSELF INTO THE COLLAPSED WRECKAGE AROUND IT."

"AS I TURNED, I SAW THESE FIREFIGHTERS GETTING READY TO GO BACK IN. THEY ALL LOOKED VERY DISTRAUGHT, BUT THE ONE ON THE LEFT REALLY CAUGHT MY EYE. HE LOOKED AS IF HE WAS HANGING HIS HEAD BECAUSE HE WAS LOST."

"It looked as if a giant hand had just crushed the whole truck right down the center, from tip to tail."

"There's a bent piece of metal that had fallen down, shearing away the traffic light, and wrapped itself around the one-way signs. It looks like cloth, but it's actually steel covered in dust."

"THIS IS ANOTHER PHOTOGRAPH I WAS NERVOUS TAKING BECAUSE THERE WERE SOLDIERS LOOKING AT ME SUSPICIOUSLY. I WAS JUST TRYING NOT TO DRAW ATTENTION TO MYSELF, EVEN THOUGH IT'S VERY HARD WHEN YOU HAVE A CAMERA UP TO YOUR EYE AND YOU'RE RECORDING SOMETHING A LOT OF PEOPLE DON'T WANT YOU TO RECORD."

"I WAS WARY OF TAKING OUT MY CAMERA AT THIS POINT BECAUSE THERE WERE SO MANY POLICE OFFICERS AROUND. THIS IS ONE OF THE FEW TIMES I SNATCHED MY CAMERA UP AND TOOK FOUR OR FIVE SHOTS AT ONCE."

By the time Woolhead made it to the Hudson River, the sun was hanging low in the sky over New Jersey. "I turned and I saw one of those F.D.N.Y. fireboats with the hoses on it. And in the back of the boat—by then the sun was starting to set—you could see these four guys, four firefighters, gathered around a barrel. They were just hanging out, chatting, cooking on the fire in the barrel, like a campfire. And in the background you could see the Statue of Liberty. It was quite an awesome sight. It sort of gave me a little bit of hope that things would get better. Because up to then it was just black and sinister and evil."

The next day, Woolhead took the rolls of film to his photo agency. He waited around while the film was developed and scanned, then sat down with an editor to see what he'd shot. "I was taken aback by how much chaos I'd captured," he recalls. "It was almost Yeatsian, you know, a terrible beauty about the photographs. They were unlike anything that any of us had ever seen."

"Just after I took this picture I was grabbed by a police officer, and she said to me, 'What do you think you're doing? Are you crazy? This is a crime scene. Get out of here!' And I said to her, in faux indignation, 'No, it's not. I'm taking photographs. This is history happening now.'"

THE MISSING

THEY WERE UBIQUITOUS, ESPECIALLY DOWNTOWN, CLUSTERED
OUTSIDE HOSPITALS, ALONG FENCES, ON LAMPPOSTS AND PHONE
BOOTHS, IN STORE WINDOWS AND SUBWAY STATIONS. SOME
WERE HASTILY SCRAWLED, AS IF OUT OF SHEER HOPELESSNESS.
OTHERS PAINSTAKINGLY PRESENTED, CHANNELING DEFIANT
OPTIMISM IN THE FACE OF IMPOSSIBLE ODDS. MOST BORE THESE
COMMON ATTRIBUTES: A PHOTO, PHYSICAL DESCRIPTION, BLOOD
TYPE, NEXT OF KIN'S CONTACT INFO (OFTEN NO MORE THAN
A LANDLINE), AND THE FLOOR THE MISSING INDIVIDUAL HAD
WORKED ON. THE HIGHER THE NUMBER, THE DEEPER THE HEART
SANK. TENS OF THOUSANDS WERE POSTED IN THE DAYS
AFTER 9/11, AND THEY ARE PERHAPS THE MOST DEVASTATING
AND INDELIBLE VISUAL LEGACY OF THAT TERRIBLE DAY.

2001

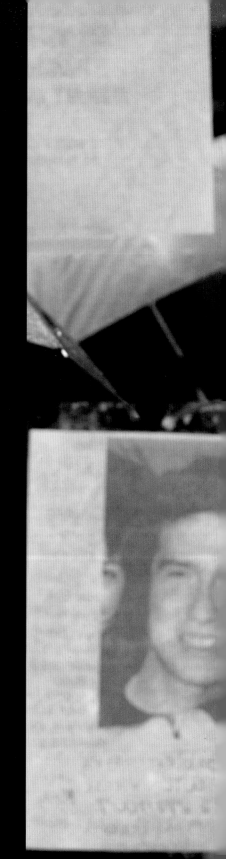

Todd Stone's painting
Towers of Light, of
the annual Tribute in Light
commemoration, 2007.

THE PAINTER

IN 1979, LANDSCAPE PAINTER TODD STONE moved into a Tribeca loft directly beneath the punk band the Plasmatics. "The reason why I am an artist in Lower Manhattan to this day," he says, "is because I could stand living under them practicing every day of the week." He sought solace on the roof of the building and often found himself gazing south over Tribeca at the Twin Towers, looming "like a mountain" at the end of West Broadway. Soon he began drawing, painting, and photographing them.

After a rainstorm on September 10, 2001, Stone took a picture out his window looking south, as he had done almost daily since the days of the Plasmatics. A little gloomy but nothing out of the ordinary for September,

Stone at work on the 67th floor of 4 World Trade Center, 2017.

"NOW IT'S CLEAR TO ME THAT THIS WAS ABOUT THE TEARS TO COME," STONE SAYS OF THE DROPLETS OF RAINWATER ALONG THE RAILINGS OF THE ADJACENT BUILDING.

droplets of rainwater collecting underneath the railings on an adjacent rooftop, Lower Manhattan's twin monoliths in the distance.

Stone is one of a handful of photographers to have captured the second plane "exploding in the viewfinder" as it hit the south tower less than 24 hours later. Instead of fleeing uptown, he went up to the roof and continued photographing and drawing the apocalyptic scene unfolding to the south. "My subject matter came to my window," he says, "and suddenly I was a history painter." He didn't stop until 7 World Trade Center collapsed late that afternoon and he and his family were forced to evacuate. They stayed with friends on 26th Street until they were allowed to return to their loft on "smoky Thomas Street" a week later. They slowly adapted to post-9/11 life downtown, a place where residents put little American flags in their windows just to indicate to the authorities that somebody still lived there, somebody was still home. "I didn't know how to access joy," Stone says of those darkest days of his life. But he and his family were determined not to leave. "Part of our decision to stay was to show that we weren't going to run."

DURING A SOMBER CEREMONY MARKING THE OFFICIAL END OF GROUND ZERO CLEANUP,

AN HONOR GUARD OF FIRST RESPONDERS SLOWLY MADE THEIR WAY UP THE 460-FOOT-LONG RAMP FROM WHAT WAS NOW A VAST VACANT PIT, 16 ACRES OF DIRT 70 FEET BENEATH STREET LEVEL. THEY CARRIED AN EMPTY STRETCHER, BLANKETED WITH AN AMERICAN FLAG, SYMBOLIZING THE SCORES OF VICTIMS NEVER FOUND. OF THE 2,753 PEOPLE WHO PERISHED HERE ON 9/11, MORE THAN A THOUSAND WOULD NEVER BE IDENTIFIED.

MAY 30TH

2002

The annual Tribute in Light's 88 spotlights brighten the night sky, September 11, 2009.

20
01

2002

2002–2003

02

MASTER PLAN

JUST THREE MONTHS AFTER 9/11, Governor George Pataki and Mayor Rudy Giuliani created the Lower Manhattan Development Corporation, to oversee—and control—the "rebuilding and revitalization" of Lower Manhattan. On May 22, the L.M.D.C. and the Port Authority awarded Manhattan architecture and urban-planning firm Beyer Blinder Belle a contract to come up with six concepts for "land-use options" for the site. The L.M.D.C.'s requisites for the master plan included a permanent memorial, a park, 11 million square feet of office space, 600,000 square feet of retail space, a hotel, cultural and civic institutions, and a transportation hub.

T

THOUGH BEYER BLINDER BELLE had earned accolades for its thoughtful restorations of historic properties such as Grand Central Terminal, its new buildings hadn't received such high marks. "The selection of the New York architecture firm Beyer Blinder Belle to design a master plan for ground zero and the financial district confirms once again that architecture will play no more than a marginal role in the redevelopment of Lower Manhattan," wrote architecture critic Herbert Muschamp in the next day's *New York Times*. "Mediocrity, the choice of this firm reminds us, is not a default mode. It is a carefully constructed reality, erected at vast public expense."

When the six Beyer Blinder Belle concepts were unveiled in mid-July, they were met with near-universal derision by architecture critics. "Their renderings seemed to show generic provincial cities," lamented *The Guardian*, "not the skyline of the most dynamic metropolis in the world." On a sweltering Saturday, some 5,000 New Yorkers flocked to the Jacob Javits Convention Center for an interactive public forum on the redevelopment of the site called "Listening to the City." Their criticisms were no less blistering. "Somewhere about two-thirds of the way through the meeting a comment showed up on the screen saying, 'I hate all these plans. They look like Albany,'" recalled L.M.D.C. site-planning committee chairman Roland Betts, the influential developer of Manhattan's Chelsea Piers and

> **"I HATE ALL THESE PLANS. THEY LOOK LIKE ALBANY."**

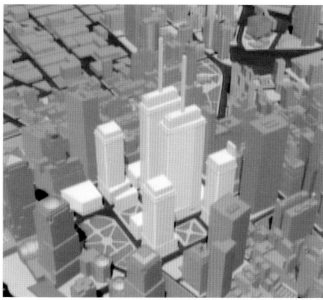

Beyer Blinder Belle's master-plan concepts were met with derision in 2002, but it's hard to deny a resemblance to the site in 2019.

consummate political insider, in 2011. "I called an emergency meeting of the L.M.D.C. and said, 'Look, we've got to scrap this thing. These plans stink, and everybody knows they stink.'"

By the end of the meeting it had been decided that the L.M.D.C. would hold an international design competition—the likes of which the world had never seen—to seek out "visionaries" from around the globe who could bring bold new ideas to the table. The guidelines were straightforward, if lofty: include a "tall symbol or structure" visible in the city skyline and "crucial to restoring the spirit of the city," preserve the footprints of the Twin Towers for memorial space, and create a transit hub with a "grand and visible station" providing "a spectacular point of arrival." Within weeks of the L.M.D.C.'s announcement of the competition, to which it had assigned the sterile title "Innovative Design Study," 406 submissions poured in from 34 countries, including entries from many of the world's leading architects and urban designers.

THE ULTIMATE PRIZE

2002–2003

BY THE END OF 2002, THE LOWER Manhattan Development Corporation had narrowed 406 applicants down to seven finalists, unveiling their master-plan design concepts at the World Financial Center's Winter Garden on December 18. The next morning, "one or more of those images was on the front page of every newspaper in the world," recalled Roland Betts.

Meier, Eisenman, Gwathmey, and Holl

Rafael Viñoly and THINK

THE SEVEN FINALISTS WERE PETERSON LITTENBERG, a small New York firm that had been consulting for the L.M.D.C.; the "Dream Team," a partnership between Richard Meier, Peter Eisenman, Charles Gwathmey, and Steven Holl; United Architects, a collaboration of architects including Greg Lynn; mega-firm Skidmore, Owings & Merrill; Rafael Viñoly's THINK team; Lord Norman Foster; and Daniel Libeskind.

The seven designs reflected very different visions, but two trends were apparant: triumphant defiance and conspicuous symbolism. Among the concepts were a "city in the sky," a bundle of intertwined, arched towers; a "vertical city" that would create a "trans-horizon" above the skyline; a "crystalline tower" whose "two halves kiss at three points"; and a "sunken garden" punctuated by two 1,400-foot spire-shaped towers.

TWO TRENDS WERE APPARENT: TRIUMPHANT DEFIANCE AND CONSPICUOUS SYMBOLISM.

Daniel
Libeskind

Skidmore,
Owings & Merrill

Lord Norman
Foster

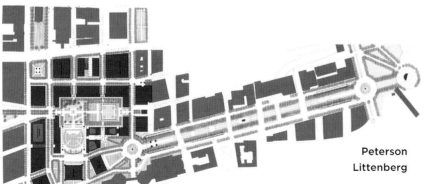

Peterson
Littenberg

United
Architects

Rafael Viñoly at the
Winter Garden, December
18, 2002. Above right:
a rendering of his design.

The public was invited to view models of the designs and submit feedback
at an exhibition at the Winter Garden. Six weeks and 8,000 comment cards
later, the L.M.D.C. narrowed the field down to two finalists: Rafael Viñoly
and Daniel Libeskind. Viñoly's design, "Towers of Culture," memorialized the
Twin Towers with two identical open latticework structures, "icons of the
Public Realm," housing cultural facilities and encasing two enormous wind
turbines. Libeskind's design, "Memory Foundations," called for preserving
a part of the pit for a "quiet, meditative and spiritual space," shadowed by a
"towering spire of 1,776 feet" with gardens filling its upper terraces.

Born in 1944 in Uruguay and raised in Argentina, Rafael Viñoly trained to
be a classical pianist before founding his first architecture firm at age 20
with six associates. He immigrated to the United States in 1979, and a prolific
career followed: more than 60 major commissions, including the iconic Tokyo

International Forum, the Edward M. Kennedy Institute, Jazz at Lincoln Center, and the 1,395-foot-tall 432 Park Avenue, the tallest residential building in the Western Hemisphere until 2019.

Two years younger than Viñoly, Daniel Libeskind was the son of Holocaust survivors who had emigrated from Poland to the Bronx in 1959. Like Viñoly, Libeskind was a classically trained musician and had once accompanied violinist Itzhak Perlman on the accordion. He spent his early career in

Daniel Libeskind shows a model of his master plan to Mayor Bloomberg and Governor Pataki.

academia studying architectural theory, and his first major commission, the Jewish Museum in Berlin, didn't come until 1989. But by the time it opened, on September 9, 2001, the museum had already brought Libeskind international acclaim.

By February 2003, Viñoly and Libeskind were battling for the biggest prize in the history of architecture, and their war of words had started to spill onto the pages of New York's tabloids. Viñoly referred to Libeskind's design as a "death pit" with a "wailing wall." Libeskind responded in kind, calling Viñoly's design "two skeletons in the sky" and even poking fun at the name of Viñoly's team, THINK. "Why the capitals?," Libeskind later wrote in his autobiography. "It seemed Orwellian, scary." As author and architecture critic Philip Nobel characterized the mêlée, "Rove-ian political tactics were taken into the world of architecture and being propagated by amateurs."

The L.M.D.C. site-planning committee voted unanimously for Viñoly's plan. The day before the winner was to be announced, the decision was leaked to *The New York Times*. PANEL SUPPORTS 2 TALL TOWERS AT DISASTER SITE, the paper reported on February 26. "Of course when I read that headline," recalled Libeskind, "I was crushed."

"ROVE-IAN POLITICAL TACTICS WERE TAKEN INTO THE WORLD OF ARCHITECTURE AND BEING PROPAGATED BY AMATEURS."

"I remember waking up in the morning and seeing on the front page of the *Times* that the L.M.D.C. is going to choose the Viñoly plan," recalled former governor George Pataki, "and going, 'No, this can't be.'" In the governor's view, Viñoly's plan was unbuildable, economically unsound, and "symbolized the destruction of the past instead of the hope of the future." Just 24 hours after the L.M.D.C. had chosen Viñoly's plan, Pataki overruled them, declaring Libeskind the de facto victor. The centerpiece of Libeskind's master plan was a symbolic 1,776-foot-tall tower he called "Gardens of the World," an asymmetrical building whose shape mimicked the Statue of Liberty and that would "rise above its predecessors, reasserting the pre-eminence of freedom and beauty." Above the commercial office space would be a "vertical park" of gardens with various "ecological zones." Topping out the tower was a massive off-center sculptural spire. During a speech to civic and business leaders on April 24, 2003, Governor Pataki branded it the "Freedom Tower," adding that his office would happily sign on as an anchor tenant. "Seventeen seventy-six is a symbol of our freedom," Pataki explained in 2012. "So it just made sense. That word just fell in and fit the building."

JUST 24 HOURS AFTER THE L.M.D.C. HAD CHOSEN VIÑOLY'S PLAN, PATAKI OVERRULED THEM, DECLARING LIBESKIND THE DE FACTO VICTOR.

20
03

2003 – 2006

"If there is to be a memorial,
let it not be of stone and steel."

— ROGER EBERT

MEMORIAL VISIONS

WITHIN DAYS OF 9/11, THE DEBATE BEGAN over what should be done with the site after the cleanup. Many were adamant that nothing should be rebuilt there—that the entire 16 acres should be a serene park, a place of quiet solitude and reflection. Lester Levine was among them. "Being an idealist, I agreed with Roger Ebert," says Levine. Ebert had published an impassioned op-ed a day after the attacks hoping for the site to become "a green field, with trees and flowers." And if there must be a memorial, he wrote, "let it not be of stone and steel."

Yaacov Agam is an Israeli artist and pioneer of "kinetic art." His design envisioned a "transformable kinetic sculpture" in the form of moving rainbows, the "universal symbol of hope and peace."

IT QUICKLY BECAME EVIDENT that a bucolic green wasn't in the cards. But in one of the few straightforward, sensible moves made by the powers that be controlling the site, it was decided that a global memorial-design competition would be held, open to anyone with access to as little as a pencil and paper. In total, 5,201 submissions poured in from 49 states and 63 countries. Sure, there were fancy CAD-software entries from architects seeking career exaltation. But the majority of entrants came from other walks of life: housewife, office manager, Great Lakes ferry captain, Vietnam refugee, husband going through a divorce who bonded with his kids by working on their submission together.

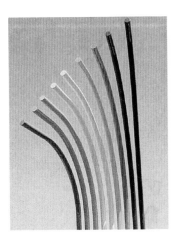

John Zissovici is a Cornell professor of architecture whose entry envisioned two fields of TV monitors, reflecting that 9/11 was a global television event. The monitors—one for each victim—would display every victim's name in "black disabled pixels ... the lost signal a reminder of the unfulfilled possibilities of each life disrupted by this catastrophic event."

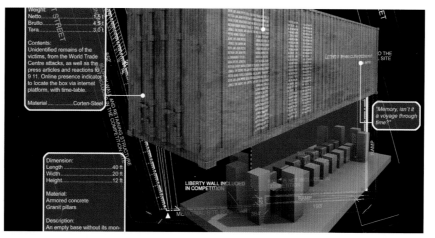

Joël Cannivé, Mark Kerger, and Stéphanie Decker envisioned a global traveling structure, visiting all 82 countries represented by the victims over 10 years. A quote on the entry frames the concept: "Memory, isn't it a voyage through time?"

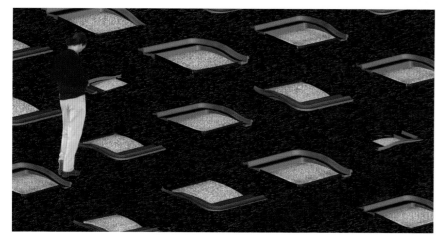

Alison Coryn is a multi-media, interdisciplinary artist who proposed using hypersonic sound technology to allow each visitor to listen to sounds and readings about 9/11.

5,201 SUBMISSIONS
POURED IN FROM 49 STATES AND 63 COUNTRIES.

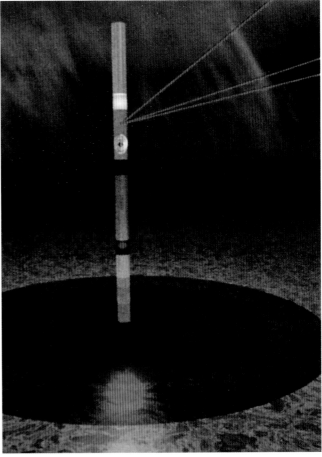

An art teacher whose family is Iraqi, Ehren Joseph envisioned lighted vertical beacons. The colored lights for each beacon would be unique to the victim being represented, through his or her "Southern Blot DNA patterns," using red, white, and blue glass lights.

Nicholas de Monchaux's entry, "Safe Passage," which he designed with an Egyptian architect friend, Omar Rabie, paid symbolic homage to New York City's maritime history with 200 boats, "each of which bears on its bulwarks the names of a dozen or more victims of the 9/11 attacks."

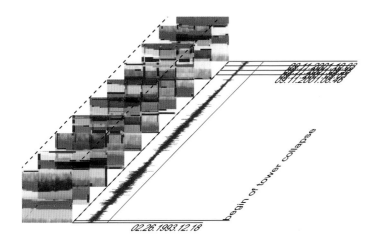

Ivy Arce is a graphic and video designer who proposed that each visitor to the 9/11 site receive a shawl with the names of the victims printed on it in the proportions of the Twin Towers. "We propose a memorial that moves beyond the physical and material and becomes a process of involvement."

Jean Pike, an architect, proposed a memorial built of sound. The architecture itself would be generated from the sound of the Twin Towers falling. As visitors walked through the memorial, they would hear the names of victims being spoken by their loved ones.

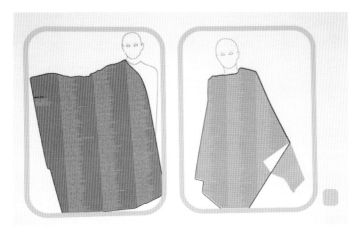

Dave Hampton Jr. and Micah Land's entry envisioned an "open-air meditative space and ossuary," with the Twin Towers' footprints as urban gardens. Their design would be a "catalyst for the creation of an authentic place for reconciliation."

Christopher Wright is the founder of an educational nonprofit. His design uses movement from a people-powered turntable to turn a spherical "World Window," which symbolizes that human beings determine the direction in which the world turns.

"AS A NATIVE NEW YORKER, I JUST WANTED TO BE PART OF IT, PART OF THE HEALING."

Lester Levine's entry was called "Evolving Memories," which aimed to challenge the memorial paradigm of "static, predictable visual and spatial experiences" with a centerpiece glass "teardrop" with randomly moving colors and sounds, each hue and tone unique to a victim.

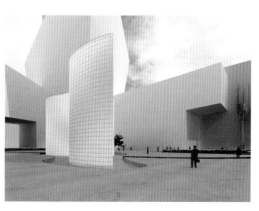

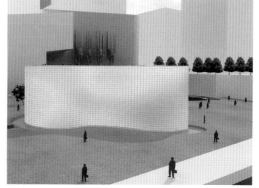

Jorn Ophee is an energy engineer from Iceland whose design envisioned a 330-foot-tall "Memorial Power Tower" with two giant turbo "wind/hydrogen Fanjet Engines [which] would produce more power than a nuclear power station," enough for all of New York City.

The 13-member memorial jury, which included representatives of the governor and mayor, victims' relatives, prominent cultural professionals, and renowned designers and architects, took six months to review all the submissions. Aside from the members of the jury, the only person to have reviewed all 5,201 entries is Lester Levine, an "organizational-change consultant" by day and a native New Yorker who was living in San Francisco at the time. "My wife and I each knew people who had died on 9/11," he says. "As a native New Yorker, I just wanted to be part of it, part of the healing." He decided to submit an entry he called "Evolving Memories," which would "challenge the memorial paradigm." Though he didn't win, the process got Levine curious about the other submissions. He spent the next seven months obsessively combing through the entries—all of which were accessible via an online archive— and taking detailed notes on each. The result was a book called *9/11 Memorial Visions*, which told the personal stories behind 137 entries that Levine considered particularly innovative or inspiring in one way or another.

An earlier version of this chapter originally appeared on vanityfair.com on September 9, 2016.

Michael Arad tested a mock-up of his memorial design on the roof of his apartment building in Manhattan's East Village.

THE MEMORIAL COMPETITION JURY had been assured that the politicians would be sidelined when it came to the memorial. Nevertheless, according to *The New York Times*, during one of their first meetings, in August 2003, they were visited in succession by Governor Pataki, Mayor Bloomberg, and former mayor Giuliani. "While Governor Pataki essentially gave the jurors a pep talk," wrote Deborah Sontag in the *Times*, "the mayor and the former mayor presented them with contrasting and irreconcilable visions of how best to honor the dead." As he had in his mayoral farewell address, Giuliani invoked "sacred ground," adding that the memorial "should be big." By contrast, Bloomberg expounded that "less is more" and advocated for a school on the site. "I always thought the best memorial for anybody is to build a better world in their memory," he said.

REFLECTING ABSENCE

20

SIX MONTHS AND 5,201 ENTRIES LATER, the jury announced the winning design. It was called "Reflecting Absence," by a 34-year-old New York City Housing Authority assistant architect named Michael Arad, who had been designing police stations for the N.Y.P.D. It was a distinct departure from the below-grade memorial Libeskind had envisioned in his master plan, which would have preserved a part of the pit as a "quiet, meditative and spiritual space" along an exposed portion of the original concrete slurry wall.

Michael Arad presenting his winning design, January 14, 2004.

"HOW DO YOU BUILD A MOMENT OF SILENCE?"

Arad's concept sprang not from the site itself but from a stone quarry he'd come across in South Orange, New Jersey. "There was just something very beautiful and evocative about it, because it had that sort of clearly traced-out absence of all the rock that had been excavated out but was softened by the water and by the trees," he recalled in 2011. "I think that helped me to start thinking about the Memorial Plaza."

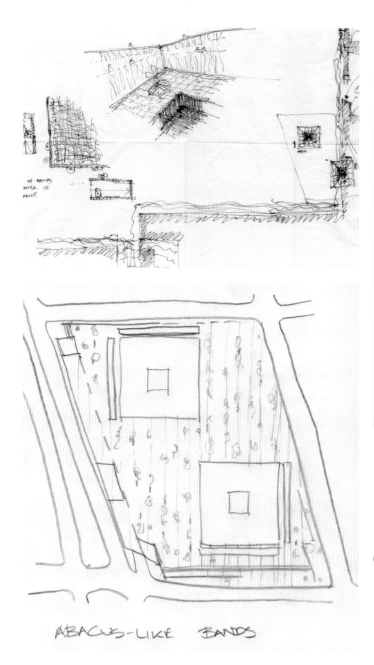

ABACUS-LIKE BANDS

After visiting the quarry, Arad created a series of sketches illustrating his concept of "twin voids."

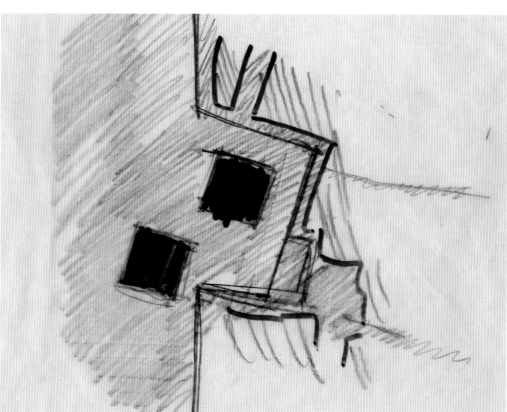

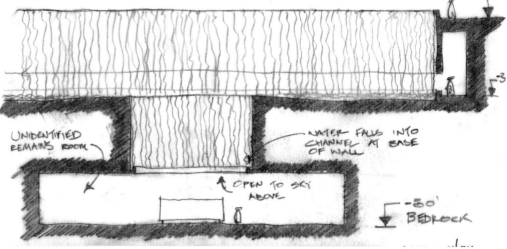

UNIDENTIFIED REMAINS ROOM

WATER FALLS INTO CHANNEL AT BASE OF WALL

OPEN TO SKY ABOVE

-3

-80' BEDROCK

ARAD'S DESIGN CONSISTED OF TWO IDENTICAL SUNKEN REFLECTING POOLS.

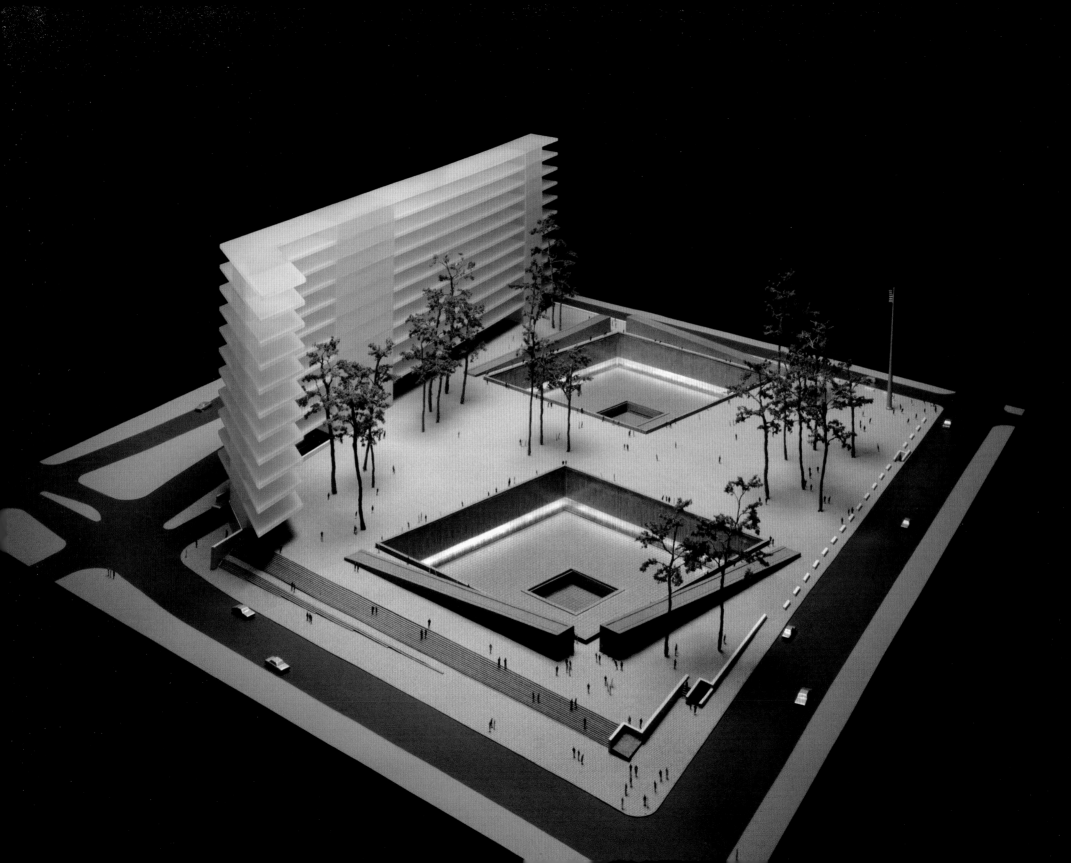

LIBESKIND ACKNOWLEDGED THE MEMORIAL'S "MEANINGFUL CONNECTION" TO HIS MASTER PLAN.

Arad's design consisted of two identical sunken reflecting pools, in the precise footprints of the Twin Towers, fed by "a constant shoot of water that cascades down the four sides of each square pit." A vast street-level plaza surrounded the pools, and visitors could descend underground to "memorial galleries" at the base of the waterfalls, where the names of the victims would be inscribed on low stone parapets. After his design was selected, Arad teamed up with landscape architect Peter Walker, who surrounded the pools with a "forest grove" of swamp white oak trees. Their collaboration was generally well received when it was unveiled on January 14, 2004. *The New York Times* called it "powerful but stark"; *New York* magazine, "bold and dignified"; *Time,* "subdued, spare and gentle." Although Arad and Walker's design was fundamentally different from his own, Libeskind nonetheless acknowledged its "meaningful connection" to his master plan.

"YOU DON'T WALK AWAY FROM IT. YOU KEEP CARING."

While many victims' families praised the design, a vocal faction quickly rose in opposition to the names being displayed underground. Rosaleen Tallon, whose brother was killed in the attacks, was among the dissenters. "You would have to descend down almost as though you were going into the subway, descend down underground into a confined space to view the names, and that shocked us," she recalled in 2011. "It's always going to be the number one target site of the terrorists." As with nearly every aspect of the rebuilding of Ground Zero, the threat of terrorism would fundamentally alter the outcome. By 2006, the powers that be had intervened, calling for the names to be raised to plaza level and displayed on 42-inch-high bronze parapets circumscribing the pools. "It felt like a tremendous blow," Arad said of the decision. "But you don't walk away from it. You stay involved. You keep caring."

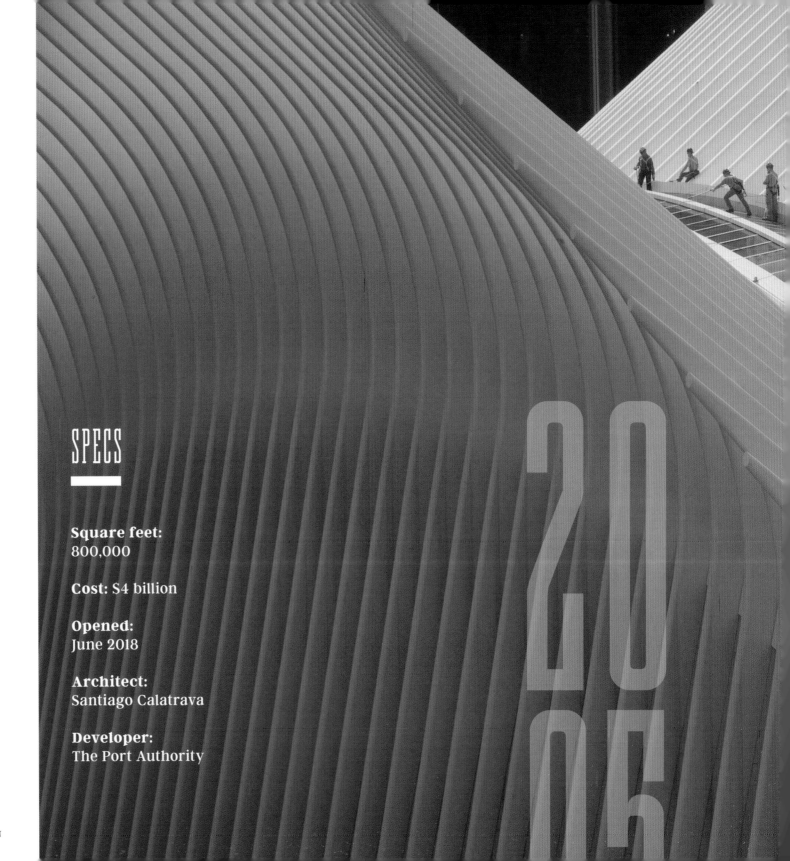

20 05

SPECS

Square feet:
800,000

Cost: $4 billion

Opened:
June 2018

Architect:
Santiago Calatrava

Developer:
The Port Authority

"The eighth wonder of the world."

—STEVE PLATE, CHIEF OF MAJOR CAPITAL
PROJECTS FOR THE PORT AUTHORITY

THE OCULUS

ON SEPTEMBER 6, 2005, Governor George Pataki, Senator Hillary Clinton, and a half-dozen other officials were all smiles as they watched architect Santiago Calatrava and his 10-year-old daughter, Sofia, release a pair of homing pigeons—"doves" symbolizing "rebirth"— to mark the groundbreaking of the new World Trade Center Transportation Hub. The exception was Mayor Michael Bloomberg, who gazed up at the birds with pursed lips and furrowed brow as if reading the tea leaves on their wings. Originally projected at $2.2 billion, the Hub would end up costing twice that—even more than the 1,776-foot-tall Freedom Tower across the plaza, the most expensive office building ever constructed—and take more than a decade to finish.

THE SPANISH-BORN CALATRAVA
is known for his curvy, avian-inspired
neo-futurist bridges and buildings—
and his soaring budgets. The City of
Arts and Sciences, a cultural complex
in his hometown of Valencia, saw its
construction budget triple to more than
$1 billion, a debilitating sum for Spain's
third-largest city. By the time the Hub
opened, on March 3, 2016, many New
Yorkers, subjected daily to the indignities

of a crumbling subway system, were
understandably vexed that the city's
18th-busiest subway station—beneath a
tourist trap of a high-end mall—could cost
$4 billion, even after they'd taken in its
breathtaking main hall. "A stupendous
waste of public funds," as one critic put it,
given that the Hub serves only a fraction
of the daily commuters that pass through
Grand Central or Penn Station, the latter
long in need of renovation.

"THIS IS MUCH MORE THAN A STATION, ISN'T IT?"

It has in turn been called a "dino carcass," a "kitschy jeu d'esprit" saturated with "maudlin sentimentalism," and the "world's most expensive subway stop." "As functionally vapid inside as it is outside," the *New York Post*'s Steve Cuozzo opined, "a void in search of a purpose." Even the Port Authority's executive director, Pat Foye, called it "a symbol of excess" before scrapping plans to hold an opening ceremony. "At first blush, Mr. Calatrava's architecture can almost— almost—make you forget what an epic boondoggle the whole thing has been," wrote Michael Kimmelman in *The New York Times* the day before it opened. Yet there was no denying the airy, snow-white grandeur of the 365-foot-long, 160-foot-tall main hall, dubbed the "Oculus."

Calatrava had first pitched his design to the public at the Winter Garden in January 2004. He sketched a picture of a child releasing a bird, then explained how the building's roof—a pair of massive

hydraulic "wings"—would open and close. "On a beautiful summer day," he told the rapt audience, "the building can work not as a greenhouse but as an open space." He got a standing ovation. Reviving site master planner Daniel Libeskind's notional "wedge of light," Calatrava

lined up the Oculus's axis so that every September 11 at exactly 10:28 A.M.—the moment the second tower collapsed— an uninterrupted ray of sunlight would span the entire length of the concourse, reflecting off the Italian Lasa-marble floors. Calatrava's hydraulic wings never

The Hub connects a dozen city subway lines and PATH trains.

took flight, but a full-length retractable skylight—composed of 224 panes of blast-resistant glass—opens once a year on September 11, weather permitting.

"New York is naturally a very beautiful place," Calatrava told *Architectural Digest* when the Oculus opened, in 2016. "I have to say, this is much more than a station, isn't it?" Steve Plate, the Port Authority executive who supervised construction, called it "the eighth wonder of the world." Perhaps *New York* magazine summed it up best: "The cost of beauty is often high."

"THE COST OF BEAUTY IS OFTEN HIGH."

OCCUPY WALL STREET

OCCUPY WALL STREET'S FIRST PROTESTERS STARTED FILLING ZUCCOTTI PARK—A THREE-QUARTER-ACRE PLAZA OWNED BY BROOKFIELD PROPERTIES AND NAMED AFTER THE COMPANY'S CIVIC-MINDED CHAIRMAN—LATE ON THE MORNING OF SEPTEMBER 17, 2011. BY THE END OF THE DAY, HUNDREDS MORE HAD ASSEMBLED, PREPARED TO SPEND THE NIGHT. EXPLOITING A ZONING-LAW LOOPHOLE, THEIR RANKS CONTINUED TO MULTIPLY OVER THE FOLLOWING WEEKS, AND EVENTUALLY THE ENTIRE PLAZA WAS A 24-7 TENT CITY COMPLETE WITH FREE MEALS, A MEDIA CENTER, LIBRARY, AND MEDICAL STATION. AT THE CORE OF THEIR MESSAGE WAS INCOME INEQUALITY, WHICH HAD REACHED LEVELS NOT SEEN IN GENERATIONS, AND THEIR SLOGAN, "WE ARE THE 99%," SOON WENT VIRAL. THE PROTESTERS WOULD OCCUPY ZUCCOTTI PARK UNTIL NOVEMBER 15, WHEN MAYOR BLOOMBERG AND THE N.Y.P.D., CITING SANITARY AND OTHER PUBLIC-SAFETY CONCERNS, EVICTED THEM.

2011

21ST
CENTURY
TOWERS

2006 - 2018

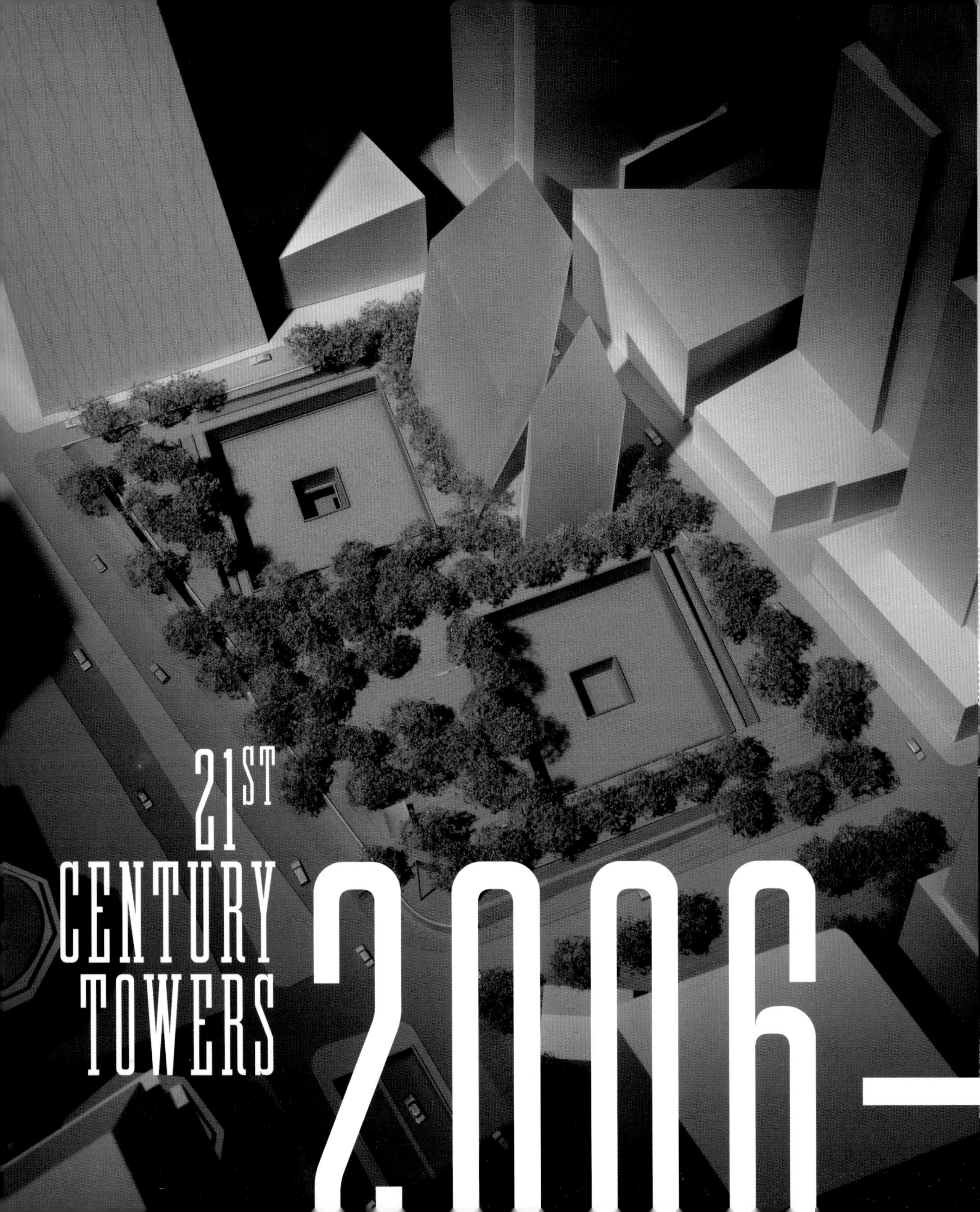

"THESE TOWERS ARE THE BEST BUILDINGS THAT HAVE EVER BEEN BUILT IN AMERICA," developer Larry Silverstein proudly declared in 2018, "because of what we learned on 9/11 about how *not* to build high-rise buildings." They're also the most expensive. One World Trade Center, formerly known as the Freedom Tower, topped out at $3.9 billion, making it the most expensive office tower ever built. Not far behind was 3 World Trade Center, at $2.7 billion. But, as the saying goes, you get what you pay for: all four of the new towers are loaded with cutting-edge safety and sustainability features, from elevators that harness the energy of gravity to rainwater collection, to pressurized stairwells and blast-resistant cable-net glass walls in the lobbies. They're among the most technologically advanced buildings ever erected and the most substantial addition to downtown's skyline since the Twin Towers.

7 WTC SPECS

Height: 741 feet

Floors: 52

Square feet:
1.7 million

Opened:
2006

Cost:
$700 million

Architect:
David Childs

Developer:
Larry Silverstein

Notable tenants:
Moody's,
the New York
Academy
of Sciences,
Fast Company

"One man's stubborn vision prevailed over pessimism and pettiness."

—STEVE CUOZZO, THE *NEW YORK POST*

RESURRECTION

"IT IS A MEASURE OF LOWER MANHATTAN'S COMPLEXITY

that a 21st-century office tower should be shaped by an 18th-century roadbed," noted David Dunlap in *The New York Times* in 2002, after plans for the new 7 World Trade Center were unveiled. Anticipating the re-establishment of Greenwich Street—which dates to the late 18th century and had been severed by the original World Trade Center's elevated "superblock"—as a bustling thoroughfare reconnecting Tribeca to the financial district, architect David Childs had canted the new building's footprint to fit the original street grid. Larry Silverstein's new, 52-story, $700 million tower was the first to open on the site four years later, on May 23, 2006, and was the city's first LEED Gold-certified "green" skyscraper.

A YEAR TO THE DAY AFTER 7 WORLD
TRADE'S RIBBON-CUTTING CEREMONY,
the biggest insurance settlement in history
was announced, marking the end of a five-
year-long legal battle between Silverstein
and eight of the two dozen companies that
had insured the Twin Towers, clearing the
last major hurdle to rebuilding the rest of the
site. In all, Silverstein collected $4.6 billion in
insurance claims. It wouldn't be nearly enough
for him to rebuild all of the square footage
lost on 9/11, but it was a good start and would
help free up another $3 billion in tax-exempt
Liberty bonds and other financing for the

Behind the lobby reception desk is a 65-foot-wide, 14-foot-tall
L.E.D. screen conceived by artist Jenny Holzer that continuously scrolls
selections of poetry and prose on a 36-hour loop.

DAVID CHILDS CANTED THE BUILDING'S FOOTPRINT TO FIT THE ORIGINAL STREET GRID.

developer. (Goldman Sachs, for its part, would get $1.7 billion in Liberty bonds to build its new headquarters across West Street.)

That the new 7 World Trade Center could be rebuilt relatively quickly had much to do with the fact that no one had died in the collapse of its predecessor, and that it had housed a vital transformer substation that Con Edison urgently needed back online. Although Silverstein initially had trouble attracting tenants, within five years the building was fully leased and neighboring 4 World Trade had nearly topped out.

The original 7 World Trade Center was designed by Emery Roth & Sons and opened in 1987.

4 WTC
SPECS

Height: 977 feet

Floors: 72

Square feet:
2.5 million

Opened:
November 2013

Cost: $1.7 billion

Architect:
Fumihiko Maki

Developer:
Larry Silverstein

Notable tenants:
Spotify, SNY,
Morningstar,
The Port Authority

*"The biggest skyscraper
New Yorkers have never heard of."*

— DAVID DUNLAP, *THE NEW YORK TIMES*, JUNE 24, 2012

SCULPTURE IN THE SKY

"WELL, IT REFLECTS MY PERSONALITY," architect Fumihiko Maki replied when asked about the "quiet dignity" of 4 World Trade Center in 2012. "No, I'm just kidding!" Humor was just one of the virtues the Pritzker Prize– winning architect drew on back in 2006 after he was given just four months to deliver plans for the 977-foot-tall tower, which he calls "a sculpture submerged within the skyline of Manhattan."

MODESTY IS ANOTHER PERSONALITY TRAIT THAT THE soft-spoken, Japanese-born Maki manifest in his design. As if by a magic trick, the building virtually vanishes into the sky when viewed from certain angles, at certain times of day, an effect achieved by using extra-thick glass to prevent the "bowing" of individual panes for a near perfectly flat, mirror-like façade.

"Deferential," "understated," "restrained," "subtle," "quiet"—all are words that have been used to describe 4 World Trade.

Maki was also acutely aware of the gravitas of the site and wanted his design to respond to it. "We wanted to make the building an homage to the memorial," he explained, "to give a certain tribute to this special place."

The 47-foot-tall, glass-faced lobby's columns are 80 feet apart, so the view out onto the memorial plaza—visited daily by an average of nearly 20,000 people from all over the world—is almost entirely unobstructed. "Upon arriving at the base of the tower, one begins to feel a sense of place, not just a piece of sculpture," Maki said. "In this way, architecture is different from pure art."

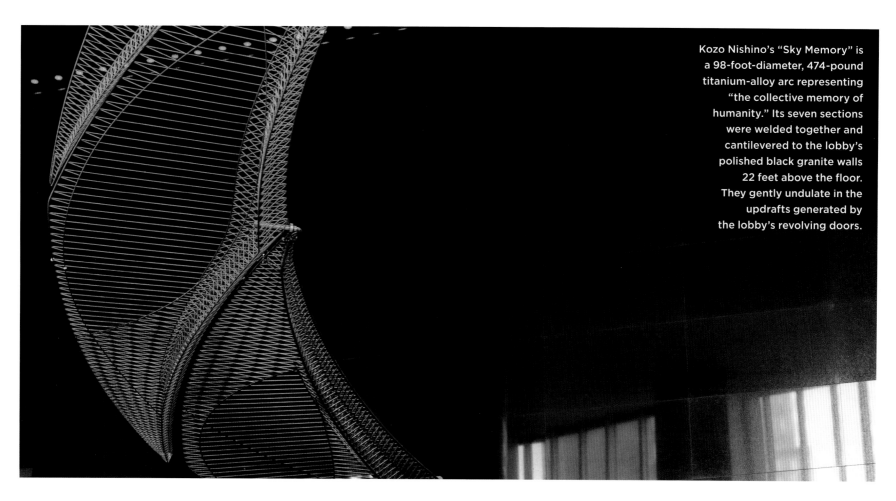

Kozo Nishino's "Sky Memory" is a 98-foot-diameter, 474-pound titanium-alloy arc representing "the collective memory of humanity." Its seven sections were welded together and cantilevered to the lobby's polished black granite walls 22 feet above the floor. They gently undulate in the updrafts generated by the lobby's revolving doors.

MAKI WANTED HIS DESIGN TO RESPOND TO
THE GRAVITAS OF THE SITE.

HOPE 4 TOMORROW /
Scott Walker

GRAFFITI ON HIGH

"YOU CAN PAINT THE CEILINGS, the floors, the walls, the windows. You can even paint the toilets," developer Larry Silverstein told the 50-plus street artists he invited to the 34,000-square-foot 69th floor of 4 World Trade in early 2013. Few surfaces were left blank. And the surprise upside? When music-streaming service Spotify was considering moving into the building, it was a casual tour of the 69th floor that sealed the deal, according to Silverstein. "When

"YOU CAN EVEN PAINT THE TOILETS," SILVERSTEIN TOLD THE ARTISTS.

they looked around, they realized that, by golly, this space was a spectacular space," he recalled. "It took the street artists to open their eyes and minds to the reality of what they had here." In early 2017, the company signed a lease for 378,000 square feet (which would later grow to nearly half a million). "Art is embedded into the corporate culture at the new World Trade Center," observed *Forbes,* crediting Silverstein with "flipping the corporate office script Silicon Valley style."

THE RISING / Joe Iurato and Chris Stain

VANDAL GUMMY BLUE & RED /
WhIsBe

16"
15"
14"
13"
12"
11"
10'
9"
8"
7"

DEPT. OF CORRECTIONS
NEW YORK, NY
6-6-07
BEAR, GUMMY

DEPT. OF CORRECTIONS
BROOKLYN, NY
6-6-07
BEAR, GUMMY

3'
2"
"
0

COSMIC TOWER /
Stickymonger

SUNSET SILVER /
Dimension Rock

*WHEN I CLOSE
MY EYES I IMAGINE
A USONIAN CITY
OF DREAMS /*
Ian Ferguson

THE CENTERPIECE of Daniel Libeskind's 2003 master plan was a symbolic, 1,776-foot-tall tower topped off by a soaring sculptural spire inspired by Lady Liberty's upstretched arm. He called it "Gardens of the World"—above the office space would be a "vertical park" of gardens—and promised it would "rise above its predecessors, reasserting the pre-eminence of freedom and beauty." Addressing a luncheon for civic and business leaders on April 24, 2003, a rhapsodic Governor George Pataki declared it the "Freedom Tower."

"Everything is a symbol at Ground Zero."

— THE DAILY NEWS

DOWNTOWN ICON

ONE WTC SPECS

Height: 1,776 feet

Floors: 104

Square feet: 3.5 million

Opened: 2014

Cost: $3.9 billion

Architect:
David Childs

Developers:
Larry Silverstein,
The Port Authority

Notable tenants:
Condé Nast,
Vantone China Center,
General Services
Administration

"OUR GROUP HAS THE RIGHT TO SELECT the architect responsible for preparing rebuilding plans," developer Larry Silverstein wrote to L.M.D.C. chairman John Whitehead, the former Goldman Sachs chief who had been installed by Governor Pataki to oversee the rebuilding process. That architect was David Childs of Skidmore, Owings & Merrill, who'd designed 7 World Trade Center and the Time Warner Center, at Columbus Circle. Silverstein had first hired Childs in 2001 to spruce up the Twin Towers. Silverstein acknowledged Libeskind's role but insisted his man be in charge. "You can't have two generals," Childs explained in 2011. "You've got to have one who has 51 percent of the vote."

A SOARING SCULPTURAL SPIRE REFLECTED
LADY LIBERTY'S UPSTRETCHED ARM.

An early sketch and model of Libeskind's master plan.

Childs essentially torqued and tapered Libeskind's design, added more office space, and swapped out the vertical park for a wind-turbine farm (irking environmentalists concerned about errant bird flocks). Libeskind derided Childs's makeover as a "giant corkscrew with a bird on top." Childs remarked of Libeskind's asymmetrical spire, "God doesn't like eccentric loads." By the end of 2003, Libeskind had all but checked out. When asked about the new design, he told a *New York Post* reporter, "I'm not the architect of this building. You have to ask Mr. Childs."

THOSE WHO LOST THEIR
ND AS A TRIBUTE TO THE
OF FREEDOM

JULY FOURTH 2004

THE CORNERSTONE

"Twenty tons of beautifully polished national disgrace." — THE DAILY NEWS

IN AN ELABORATE, politically charged ceremony on July 4, 2004, less than two months before the Republican National Convention would roll into Midtown, a 20-ton Adirondack-granite "cornerstone" was lowered by crane into the spot where the Freedom Tower was to supposedly rise. "Today we lay the cornerstone for a new symbol of the city and of this country and of our resolve to triumph in the face of terror," Governor Pataki gushed to the assembled reporters, public officials, and victims' families. "Today we build the Freedom Tower."

When Pataki, New Jersey governor Jim McGreevey, and Mayor Bloomberg assembled for the all-important photo op, Larry Silverstein "went with the flow," joining the three politicians in front of the gleaming stone. According to Janno Lieber, Silverstein's executive in charge of rebuilding, Pataki's aides were furious at Silverstein for "ruining the shot." "It was just a reminder at the time that they had mixed feelings about private developers being part of this story," Lieber recalled in 2011, "even though we were the ones who were building the buildings!"

Two years later, construction had yet to begin. The cornerstone remained at the side of the pit, ignominiously covered by a blue plywood box. In the pre-dawn hours of June 23, 2006, it was quietly loaded onto a flatbed truck, draped with a tarp, and driven back to the Hauppauge, Long Island, headquarters of the stone company that had engraved it. "Twenty tons of beautifully polished national disgrace," the *Daily News* lamented, had become a symbol of all that had gone wrong with the redevelopment effort. "No one made a speech this morning," noted David Dunlap in *The New York Times*. "No one sang 'God Bless America.' No one read from the Declaration of Independence."

From left: Larry Silverstein, Governor Pataki, Mayor Bloomberg, and New Jersey governor Jim McGreevey, July 4, 2004.

Nine months after the cornerstone ceremony, the N.Y.P.D. ruled that the base of the tower—which sloped gently outward toward West Street—was too vulnerable to vehicular bombs. Childs's solution was to shrink and square the building's base, thus "moving" it 40 feet further from the street without actually moving it. Instead of a glass curtain wall, the base would now be made of three-foot-thick reinforced concrete and rise 15 stories, earning it the descriptors "bunker" and "fortress." Despite the redesign, Silverstein, in April 2006, after prolonged negotiations, agreed to hand over control of the Freedom Tower to the Port Authority in exchange for the right to build towers 2, 3, and 4 on the more desirable east side of the site.

On December 17, 2006, another ceremony marked another milestone: the arrival of the Freedom Tower's first steel column. Forged at the Arcelor mill in Differdange, Luxembourg, and finished at Banker Steel in Lynchburg, Virginia, at 25 tons and 31 feet long it was one of the biggest ever made. Dignitaries and 9/11 victims' families assembled to write messages on it before it was lowered into the tower's foundation two days later (prompting yet another ceremony). "This steel symbolizes the resiliency of our great city," declared Mayor Bloomberg. "This beam is not only supporting a physical building," Daniel Libeskind told a *New York Times* reporter, "it's supporting the spirit of America." Symbolic ceremonies proliferated as the public grew increasingly impatient with the glacial pace of progress on the site. "Everything is a symbol at Ground Zero," in the words of an exasperated *Daily News* reporter.

In 2009, the Freedom Tower was rebranded the flaccid, if less ostentatious, "One World Trade Center," and a year later magazine publisher Condé Nast signed a tentative deal to become its anchor tenant. "Think: Anna Wintour, the imperious editor-in-chief of Condé Nast's Vogue, who inspired the novel and film 'The Devil Wears Prada,' and Graydon Carter, the bon vivant editor of Vanity Fair, stepping out of black limousines at ground zero," marveled Charles Bagli in the *Times*. It would be another four years until the company moved in, but it was a major turning point for One World Trade and a bellwether in the evolution of downtown from the financial district to the home of a diverse array of companies, many big-media and technology firms.

Workers lowered the
Freedom Tower's first steel
column into place on
December 19, 2006.

The Freedom Tower would eventually employ thousands of construction workers from dozens of trades and unions as it rose skyward at the breakneck pace of a floor per week. Not a single worker was killed in the process. By contrast, nine workers died building the Twin Towers, according to *The New York Times.*

On May 10, 2013, One World Trade's signature spire was hoisted and bolted onto the tower's roof, a metaphorical punctuation mark on a tumultuous decade-long saga. "This milestone at the World Trade Center site symbolizes the resurgence and resilience of our state and our nation," proclaimed Andrew Cuomo, the fourth New York State governor to preside over the rebuilding.

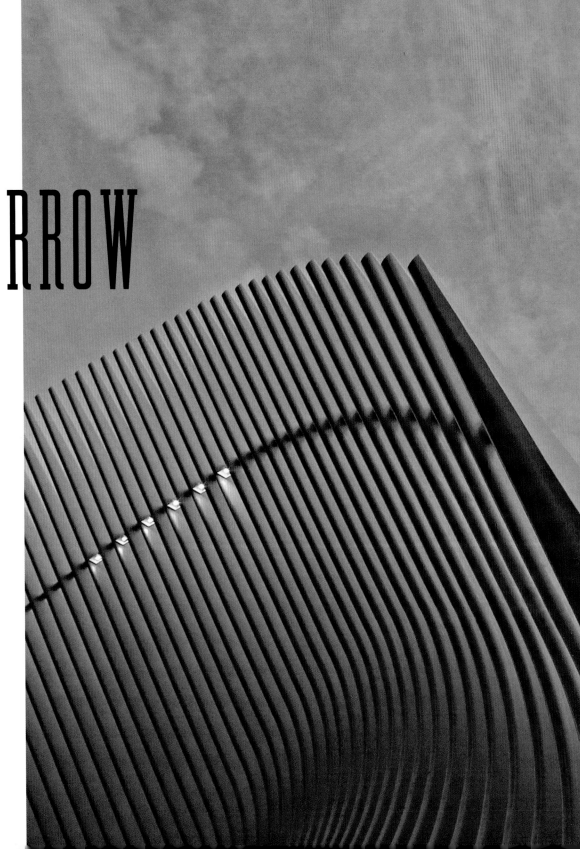

OFFICE OF TOMORROW

"WHEN YOU LOOK AT THE FAÇADE, you see the structural steel that holds the building up," developer Larry Silverstein explained in 2018. "It's the farthest thing from minimalism." Instead of conventional internal columns, structural loads are borne by a distinctive steel framework running up the exterior of the tower. In other words, architect Richard Rogers and his team made the structural architectural so that tenants could build out their spaces without having to navigate around obtrusive columns.

3 WTC SPECS

Height: 1,079 feet

Floors: 80

Square feet: 2.5 million

Cost: $2.7 billion

Opened: June 2018

Architect: Richard Rogers

Developer: Larry Silverstein

Notable tenants: GroupM, McKinsey & Company, IEX

3 World Trade Center opening ceremony, June 11, 2018. From left: Gary LaBarbera, Congresswoman Carolyn Maloney, Kevin O'Toole, Rick Cotton, Marty Burger, Tal Kerret, Lisa Silverstein, Roger Silverstein, Larry Silverstein, Richard Paul, and Kelly Clark.

ROGERS'S TEAM HAD TO IMPROVISE to reach the high bar set by Silverstein, who had demanded superlative standards of safety and sustainability. Among the innovations was a special coating on the surface of the windows that helps regulate absorption of the sun's energy. The tower also far exceeds New York City's building code for life safety, according to Silverstein. "These are the best buildings that have ever been built in America because of what we learned on 9/11."

But back in 2009, the nadir of the Great Recession, construction on 3 World Trade had ground to a halt. The Port Authority

RICHARD ROGERS AND HIS TEAM MADE THE STRUCTURAL ARCHITECTURAL.

Media agency GroupM signed on as anchor tenant in 2013 and now has 4,000 employees working in 700,000 square feet of futuristic, award-winning office space.

proposed that Silverstein shrink it to a squat four-story "stump," housing a handful of retail outlets. But Silverstein persisted and eventually landed anchor tenant GroupM, the world's largest media-investment firm, unlocking $1.3 billion in Liberty-bond financing. "The curtain went up," as Silverstein recalled, and construction resumed. In June 2016, the building topped out at 1,079 feet, making it the fifth-tallest skyscraper in the city.

"A cross between deconstructionism with a willful asymmetry and neo-modernism with a mid-century corporate flare," noted *The Real Deal* of the design, "that looks as though it came straight out of the Mad Men era." While it isn't difficult to conjure Don Draper striding through its sleek, four-story-tall glass lobby, the building also had to respond to the needs of millennials,

3 World Trade Center's 17th-floor terrace.

for whom sustainability and lifestyle amenities are tick-the-box requisites. The new generation of office worker expects such luxuries as "curated amenity spaces" or, as Silverstein put it, "places that foster creativity where young people would want to work and collaborate." Think coffee bars, terraces, performance venues, makerspaces, and—wait for it—virtual-reality lounges surrounded by floor-to-ceiling graffiti art. Welcome to the office of tomorrow.

IT ISN'T DIFFICULT TO CONJURE DON DRAPER STRIDING THROUGH THE LOBBY.

The B. Fischer & Co. Building at 375 Greenwich Street in the 1940s and 2005 (right).

TRIANGLE BELOW CANAL

"ONCE KNOWN AS WASHINGTON MARKET, the area was rechristened TriBeCa (for Triangle Below Canal) in 1974 by an undoubtedly whimsical geographer at the Office of Lower Manhattan Development," wrote Andrew Yarrow in *The New York Times* in 1985. "Less touristy than SoHo, with fewer boutiques, TriBeCa has maintained its raw quality complete with food and textile wholesalers, gritty warehouses, ungentrified neighborhood bars, and century-old cast-iron buildings." Four years later, actor and local resident Robert De Niro, fresh off *Goodfellas*, bought a 50 percent share in the nearly century-old B. Fischer & Co. coffee warehouse at 375 Greenwich Street and opened the Tribeca Film Center and Grill. In the wake of 9/11, De Niro launched the Tribeca Film Festival, which would eventually grow into one of the country's leading festivals, attracting nearly half a million attendees. Gone are the textile wholesalers and ungentrified bars. The 75-year-old Oscar-winning actor's neighbors now include Justin Timberlake and Jessica Biel, Beyoncé and Jay-Z—among other glitterati—and by 2017 the neighborhood's 10007 Zip Code had become the city's richest.

LOWER MANHATTAN'S RESIDENTIAL POPULATION HAS TRIPLED to more than 62,000 people since 9/11, according to the Downtown Alliance. A total of 1,300 new apartment units became available in 2018. Twenty-seven percent of people who live downtown also work there, "the highest work-live ratio in the United States," according to Larry Silverstein, who moved into a penthouse at 30 Park Place, one of his firm's developments, in May 2018.

The 76-story, 904-unit 8 Spruce Street, designed by Frank Gehry, features an undulating stainless-steel façade. In the March 7, 2011, issue of *The New Yorker,* Paul Goldberger called it "one of the most beautiful towers downtown" and the "first thing built downtown since then that actually deserves to stand beside [the Woolworth Building]."

"The Financial District is over," wrote the *New York Post*'s Steve Cuozzo in 2007. "But say hello to FiDi, the coinage of major downtown landlord Kent Swig, who decided it's time to humanize the old F.D. with an easily remembered, fun-sounding acronym." Fun as it sounded, within a decade it would be obsolete. People who work downtown increasingly do so for so-called TAMI—technology, advertising, media, and information—companies. By 2018, the financial industry represented just a third of the pie, down from 56 percent in 2000.

The 792-foot-tall Woolworth Building, which architecture critic Paul Goldberger once called "the Mozart of skyscrapers," was the tallest building in the world for almost two decades after it opened in 1913. The top 30 floors were converted to luxury condos between 2012 and 2019.

The 82-story 30 Park Place, designed by Robert A. M. Stern to look as if it could have been built a century ago, opened in 2016 and includes residences and a Four Seasons hotel. "If you look far enough," developer Larry Silverstein told the *Times* of the view from his 80th-floor terrace, "you can see the curvature of the earth."

The building's residential lobby features a black-granite and Thassos-marble floor, a silver-leaf rotunda ceiling, and a polished onyx fireplace.

IMAGINING THE FUTURE

"IF IN WESTEROS IT IS WINTER THAT IS COMING," wrote architect Mark Foster Gage in 2017, "in Manhattan it's water. Lots of it." Gage's "East River Valley" was one of nine proposals commissioned by *New York* magazine, which asked "some of New York City's most innovative architects how they'd like to fix this place up a bit." East River Valley was among the boldest: why not drain the East River, revealing "a beautiful and fertile valley awaiting rescue"? After all, the East River isn't actually a river at all, Gage pointed out, but a tidal strait, a "flood prone pseudo-river." Aside from helping to mitigate the impact of storm surges with three "strategically placed" dams, Gage's 15,000-acre "infrastructure-free" urban valley would include farms, parks, gardens, and "geothermal wells to power the next century of New York City's energy needs."

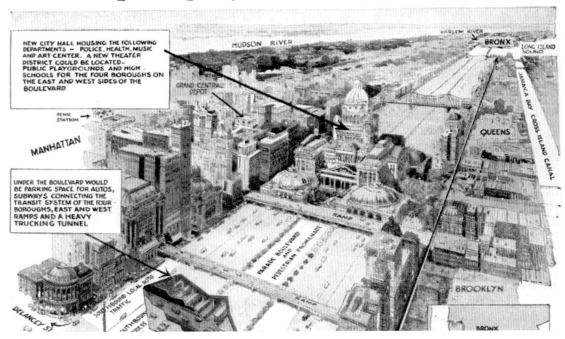

December, 1924   *POPULAR SCIENCE MONTHLY*   47

Plan to Drain a New York River

Vast Engineering Project to Relieve Traffic Congestion

NEW CITY HALL HOUSING THE FOLLOWING DEPARTMENTS — POLICE, HEALTH, MUSIC AND ART CENTER. A NEW THEATER DISTRICT COULD BE LOCATED. PUBLIC PLAYGROUNDS AND HIGH SCHOOLS FOR THE FOUR BOROUGHS ON THE EAST AND WEST SIDES OF THE BOULEVARD

UNDER THE BOULEVARD WOULD BE PARKING SPACE FOR AUTOS, SUBWAYS CONNECTING THE TRANSIT SYSTEM OF THE FOUR BOROUGHS, EAST AND WEST RAMPS AND A HEAVY TRUCKING TUNNEL

HARLEM RIVER   HUDSON RIVER   BRONX   LONG ISLAND SOUND   GRAND CENTRAL DEPOT   PENN. STATION   MANHATTAN   QUEENS   JAMAICA BAY CROSS ISLAND CANAL   RAMP   PARADE BOULEVARD AND PEDESTRIAN PROMENADE   BROOKLYN   DELANCEY ST.   NORTHBOUND LOCAL AUTO TRAFFIC   SOUTHBOUND EXPRESS   BRONX

IT WASN'T THE FIRST TIME a starry-eyed, urban-planning visionary had proposed draining the East River. The notion can be traced back to at least 1924, when *Popular Science Monthly* illustrated its "Plan to Drain a New York River." Instead of a bucolic green valley, *Popular Science*'s scheme had a decidedly more utilitarian purpose: relieve traffic congestion. The East River would be drained and dammed by concrete retaining walls at each end. A five-mile-long central "parade boulevard and pedestrian promenade" would run down the middle, flanked by dozens of lanes of local and express traffic and anchored by a new city

THE EAST RIVER ISN'T ACTUALLY A RIVER AT ALL.

FILLING in the HUDSON

This map vividly tells the story of the plan to dam the Hudson river and rebuild New York, ending the isolation of Manhattan Island. Water which now finds an outlet through Hudson river would be diverted via widened Harlem river to the East river and then into outer harbor. What is new Manhattan Island would be grafted to New Jersey.

by ALFRED ALBELLI

PLUG up the Hudson river at both ends of Manhattan . . . divert that body of water into the Harlem river so that it might flow out into the East river and down to the Atlantic ocean . . . pump out the water from the area of the Hudson which has been dammed off . . . fill in that space . . . ultimately connecting the Island of Manhattan with the mainland of New Jersey . . . and you have the world's eighth wonder—the reconstruction of Manhattan!

That is the essence of the plan proposed by Norman Sper, noted publicist and engineering scholar. It is calculated to solve New York City's traffic and housing problems, which are threatening to devour the city's civilization like a Frankenstein monster.

In keeping with the Norman Sper plan, the ten square miles of land which would thereby be reclaimed from the Hudson would not only provide for thousands of additional buildings, but also for avenues and cross streets which would greatly relieve the congestion in present thoroughfares.

Today there are ten avenues laid out along the length of Manhattan. These are crossed by 125 streets. It is the lack of up-and-down arteries which has given rise to the existing traffic crisis. Sper would double the number of avenues.

Foundation for New Buildings

His suggestions go still further. No use waiting, he says, until the entire area is filled in before starting underground improvements. Build your tunnels, conduits, mail and automobile tubes, and other subterranean passages indispensable to comfort in the biggest city in the universe as you go along. Do it in the process of filling the basin left by the drawing off of the water.

"When every possible subterranean necessity had been anticipated and built," Sper points out, "a secondary fill would bring the level up to within twenty-five feet of the Manhattan street level.

"Upon this level would rest the foundations and basements of the buildings that would make up the new city above, planned

Modern Mechanix and

Map and perspective drawing of the project. The Harlem River would provide a ship waterway from the Hudson to Long Island Sound, while a canal would give access to Jamaica Bay and the Atlantic Ocean

hall and "theater district" at the midpoint. Beneath the boulevard would be a network of subways, parking garages, east-west ramps, and a "heavy trucking tunnel."

It wasn't just the East River that the visionaries proposed plugging. Alfred Albelli, writing in the March 1934 issue of *Modern Mechanix and Inventions* magazine, described a plan "calculated to solve New York City's traffic and housing problems, which are threatening to devour the city's civilization like a Frankenstein monster," by damming and filling in the Hudson from the Battery to the Harlem River, thereby "ending the isolation of Manhattan Island."

But back to storm surges. In 2012, Hurricane Sandy pushed a nine-foot deluge into Lower Manhattan, flooding many downtown lobbies to waist level and knocking out power to all but Battery Park City. The surge also swamped the underground, and still under construction, 9/11 Memorial Museum, destroying much of the recent

Design firm DLANDstudio proposed a system of wetlands and marshes to mitigate storm surges.

electrical and drywall work and leaving a seven-foot-deep pool of fetid greenish-black water. Power wasn't fully restored to the neighborhood for nearly a week.

Since Sandy, dozens of proposals to protect Lower Manhattan from the next big one have been floated: floodwalls, dams, dunes, shoals, pumps, berms, levees, marshland. But by 2019 the only conspicuous defense measures yet deployed were "glorified sandbags," hardly reassuring to the New Yorkers living and working behind them. "Six years of studying it and you come up with sandbags? Really?" one South Street business owner told *The New York Times* in May 2019. "Officials have admitted that they do not have a plan for protecting much of the financial district," the paper reported. "They have concluded that Lower Manhattan is simply too congested, with 18 subway lines and a tangle of utilities running beneath its warren of narrow streets."

Storm surge from Hurricane Sandy flooding the World Trade Center site, October 29, 2012.

SINCE HURRICANE SANDY, DOZENS OF PROPOSALS TO PROTECT LOWER MANHATTAN FROM THE NEXT BIG ONE HAVE BEEN FLOATED.

Naming rights for the Ronald O. Perelman Center for the Performing Arts were secured by the business magnate in 2016 for $75 million. The center is expected to be completed in 2021 and will include innovative features such as adaptable theater spaces and a translucent-marble exterior.

"THIS IS NOT ROME, a great historic monument to hold as it is, but something which evolves and changes," architect David Childs told me in 2011. "That's the nature of New York." Yet, to wander Lower Manhattan, where uptown's tidy street grid yields to a tangle of lanes and alleyways, many dating to the 1600s, isn't entirely unlike exploring the side streets of Rome, where one might stumble upon, say, Via del Piè di Marmo's giant first-century marble foot, one of my personal favorites. In short order, Lower Manhattan's wanderer might find herself staring down Arturo Di Modica's *Charging Bull*; or taking in the colorful Beaux-Arts archways of the Battery Maritime Building; or gazing up at the ornamental ironwork on the imposing neo-Renaissance Federal Reserve Bank of New York Building, said to have been inspired by Florentine palazzos Strozzi and Vecchio; or strolling among the centuries-old tombstones in the graveyard behind St. Paul's Chapel, the city's oldest public building, in the shadow of Santiago Calatrava's Oculus, one of its newest.

In 1963, the demolition of the original McKim, Mead & White–designed Pennsylvania Station, whose soaring Doric-columned waiting hall had been modeled on Rome's Baths of Caracalla and Diocletian, outraged the public and galvanized preservationists. "We will probably be judged not by the monuments we build," Ada Louise Huxtable lamented, "but by those we have destroyed." In response, the New York City Council passed the Landmarks Preservation Law, the first of its kind in the country. "For generations, New Yorkers embraced the mantra of change," *The New York Times*'s Michael Kimmelman later wrote, "assuming that what replaced a beloved building would probably be as good or better." Hundreds of thousands of commuters have suffered its replacement daily since, "a subterranean rat's maze" and an embarrassment to any

"CHANGE IS THE ONLY CONSTANT." — HERACLITUS

civilized modern metropolis. "A rich and powerful city, noted for its resources of brains, imagination and money," Huxtable concluded, "could not rise to the occasion." (For all of its $4 billion, Calatrava's Oculus at least rises to *something*, even if it hasn't yet found its occasion.)

The city's newly created Landmarks Preservation Commission declared Grand Central Terminal a landmark in 1967, calling it "one of the great buildings of America." Yet that didn't keep the Penn Central Company from trying to build a 56-story office tower atop it a year later. In 1977, the commission designated South Street Seaport a historic district, citing its "richness, diversity and great historical significance." Yet that, too, hasn't kept developers from encroaching. Local residents and preservationists recently defeated plans for a 52-story "anywheresville tower that will drain the life out of [the district] like some weed that overshadows all the small plants," as one of them told the *Times*. "People go down to the Seaport because it speaks to our collective memory, our collective thoughts about what is New York City."

Despite existential threats, many of downtown's historic buildings *have* been saved—if not by law, by love (and, of course, money). The Woolworth Building, "the Mozart of skyscrapers," wasn't granted landmark status by the city until 1983, but that didn't keep its owner from carefully restoring the original terra-cotta and limestone façade in the late 1970s. "I can't think of anything comparable in the city," the Landmarks Preservation Commission's chairman noted, "in which one management has been so long associated with a building and has lavished so much care and attention on it." The Equitable Building, the impetus behind the city's 1916 Zoning Resolution, didn't receive landmark status until 1996, but that didn't keep developer Larry Silverstein from meticulously restoring many of its historic features after he bought it in 1980. New York isn't Rome, but its significant structures and districts—as historically rich, if not as old, as Rome's—are just as worthy of preservation.

"Downtowns are more than economic engines," distinguished urbanist Alexander Garvin, who was the lead planner for the Lower Manhattan Development Corporation after 9/11, wrote in his 2019 book, *The Heart of the City*. "They are repositories of knowledge and culture; they are generators of new ideas, new technology, and new ventures." But vibrant, healthy downtowns also need to balance residential and commercial, old and new. On all counts, the crown jewel of this great city has been going in the right direction since 9/11. Let's keep it that way. After all, as Garvin wrote, "cities do not change themselves." People change them.

PHOTO CREDITS/SOURCES

A&M Records

Adidas

Agnes Denes, Courtesy Leslie Tonkonow Artworks + Projects, New Yor k

Alamy Stock Photo / Angelo Hornak

Alamy Stock Photo / Erik Fuller Photography

Alamy Stock Photo / Hufton+Crow-VIEW

Alamy Stock Photo / Moviestore Collection Ltd

Alamy Stock Photo / Patti McConville

Alamy Stock Photo / Prisma by Dukas Presseagentur GmbH

Alamy Stock Photo / Shawshots

Alamy Stock Photo / ZUMA Press, Inc.

American Association for State and Local History

Andy Blair

AP Photo

AP Photo / Mary Altaffer

AP Photo / Anthony Camerano

AP Photo / Dean Cox

AP Photo / Richard Drew

AP Photo / Tina Fineberg

AP Photo / Dima Gavrysh

AP Photo / John Minchillo

AP Photo / Dave Pickoff

Michael Arad

Archpartners

Beyer Blinder Belle Architects & Planners LLP

Brooklyn Public Library, Brooklyn Collection

DLANDstudio

Downtown Lower Manhattan Association

Foster + Partners

Getty

Getty / Slim Aarons

Getty Images / AFP

Getty / Archive Photos

Getty / Bettmann

Getty / Stephen Chernin

Getty / Timothy A. Clary

Getty / Corbis Historical

Getty / Fox Photos

Getty / Frances McLaughlin-Gill

Getty / George Rinhart

Getty / Gordon Parks

Getty / Ernst Haas

Getty / Heritage Images

Getty / Hirz

Getty / Stan Honda

Getty / Hulton Archive

Getty / Peter Kramer

Getty / Lee Lockwood

Getty / Jeffrey Markowitz

Getty / *New York Daily News*

Getty / *New York Daily News* Archive

Getty / The New York Historical Society

Getty / *New York Post* Archives

Getty / Paramount Pictures

Getty / Photo 12

Getty / PhotoQuest

Getty / Scott McPartland

Getty / Joe Raedle

Getty / Smith Collection / Gado

Getty / swim ink 2 llc

Getty / Mario Tama

Getty / Allan Tannenbaum

Getty / Tony Linck

Getty / Topical Press Agency

Getty / Topical Press Agency / Hulton Archive

Getty / Transcendental Graphics

Getty / Underwood Archives

Getty / Julian Wasser

Getty / Weegee (Arthur Fellig) / International Center of Photography

© Wolfgang Hoyt / Esto

Matt Kapp

Steve Kelley aka mudpig

Kelsy Chauvin

Landmarks Preservation Commission - Carl Forster

Lester Levine

Library of Congress

Library of Congress / Getty

Magnum Photo / Danny Lyon

Mario Tama / Getty

Mark Foster Gage Architects

MOHAI, Seattle Post-Intelligencer Collection, 1986.5.2622.2

MOHAI, Seattle Post-Intelligencer Collection, 1986.5.45157

Courtesy of the Moise A. Khayrallah Center for Lebanese Diaspora Studies

Museum of the City of New York

Museum of the City of New York / Berenice Abbott (1898-1991) for Federal Art Project

Museum of the City of New York / Wurts Bros.

National Archives

National Park Service, Manhattan Historic Sites Archive

New York City Municipal Archives

New York Daily News

New York Department of Buildings,

Borough of Manhattan

Manuscripts and Archives Division, The New York Public Library. "A preposterous scheme" The New York Public Library Digital Collections. 1939.

Irma and Paul Milstein Division of United States History, Local History and Genealogy, The New York Public Library. "Manhattan: Washington Street - Rector Street" The New York Public Library Digital Collections. 1929 – 1930.

Rare Book Division, The New York Public Library. "The Bankers Club of America" The New York Public Library Digital Collections.

Billy Rose Theatre Division, The New York Public Library. "Publicity photo of Milton "Zeppo" Marx, Julius "Groucho" Marx, Leonard "Chico" Marx, and Arthur "Harpo" Marx in the motion picture *The Cocoanuts*. The New York Public Library Digital Collections. 1929.

The Miriam and Ira D. Wallach Division of Art, Prints and Photographs: Photography Collection, The New York Public Library. "Lebanon Restaurant (Syrian), 88 Washington Street, Manhattan." The New York Public Library Digital Collections. 1936.

The Miriam and Ira D. Wallach Division of Art, Prints and Photographs: Photography Collection, The New York Public Library. "Radio Row, Cortlandt Street, Manhattan." The New York Public Library Digital Collections. 1936.

The New York Times

New-York Tribune

The Ronald O. Perelman Performing Arts Center

Polaris

Popular Science

Port Authority of New York

and New Jersey

Jock Pottle

Redux / Neal Boenzi / *The New York Times*

Redux / James Estrin / *The New York Times*

Redux / Michael Evans / *The New York Times*

Redux / Don Hogan Charles / *The New York Times*

Redux / Jack Manning / *The New York Times*

Redux / Ting-Li Wang / *The New York Times*

Redux / Ruby Washington / *The New York Times*

Sesame Street Magazine

Silverstein Properties

Skidmore, Owings & Merrill (SOM)

Courtesy of the Department of Special Collections, Stanford University Libraries

© Ezra Stoller / Esto

© Ezra Stoller / Esto for the Liberty Plaza

Studio Libeskind

© David Sundberg / Esto

SyrianHistory

Ullstein Bild Dtl./Getty

Underwood Archives/Getty

University Historic Photograph Collection, Colorado State University, Archives and Special Collections

Walter P. Reuther Library, Archives of Labor and Urban Affairs, Wayne State University

Lois Weiss

Joe Woolhead

CREDITS

Written by

MATT KAPP

Edited by

DARA McQUILLAN
and **MIKE MARCUCCI**

Design Director

CHRIS MUELLER

Photo Editor

AMY BROWN

Copy Editor

ADAM NADLER

Production Director

MARYL SWICK

Associate Designers

ANTHONY ELDER
TAYLOR REAVES

Photography Consultant

JOE WOOLHEAD

ACKNOWLEDGMENTS

VERY SPECIAL THANKS:

Craig Cohen

David Friend

Jeremy Moss

Jessica Schoenholtz

Larry and Klara Silverstein

Will Luckman

SPECIAL THANKS:

Aisling Gregory

AJ Arlauckas

Alice Greenwald

Andy Breslau

Ann Schneider

Anna Colavecchio

Anthony Ribando

Bill Dacunto

Bobby Grandone

Bud Perrone

Carlos Valverde

Carol Willis

Cathy Blaney

Chad McCabe

Christina Alverado

Colette Bosque

Community Board One

Conrad Stojak

Core Twelve

David Worsley

Eija Öhrnberg

Elina Veyber

Emily Efraimov

Emma Beuster

Eric Himmel

Gianna Frederique

Glenn Plaskin

Guy Vardi

Janno Lieber

Jean Faragoi

Jeanette Oliver

Jessica Lappin

Jon Knipe

Justin Brown

Kelsy Chauvin

Lana Kovalenko

Lisa Silverstein

Lucy Kovalenko

Luisa Colón

Marty Burger

Mary Ann Tighe

Michael Bloomberg

Mickey Kupperman

Molly Mikuljan

Nygel Obama

Rachel Kraus

Rebecca Shalomoff

Richard Drutman

Robert Marcucci

Roger Silverstein

Sebastian Florin Tudor

Shari Natovitz

Stefanie Moreo

Tal Kerret

Ten Gibbs

The City of New York

The Port Authority of
New York & New Jersey

The State of New Jersey

The State of New York

Todd Stone

Tom Kluepfel

THE EDITORS

MATT KAPP is an award-winning filmmaker and writer based in Brooklyn. Most recently he wrote and co-produced the critically acclaimed documentary *16 Acres*, which told the inside story of the struggle to rebuild ground zero in the decade after 9/11. Among his other producing credits are *Valentino: The Last Emperor* and *The Education of Gore Vidal*. Aside from his film and television work, he was a reporter-researcher and web contributor for *Vanity Fair* for more than 15 years and has written frequently for *Downtown* magazine. He is a graduate of New York University's Tisch School of the Arts and a native of Burlington, Vermont.

MIKE MARCUCCI has worked in the entertainment industry for over 20 years and has been filming all aspects of design, development and construction of the World Trade Center project since 2004. He produced the award-winning documentary *16 Acres*, which the *New York Post* called a "riveting and emotional" look at one of the most complex urban-renewal projects in American history. Prior to that, he worked for Troma Films, Universal Pictures, MTV, VH1, CBS, New Line Cinema, Robert De Niro's Tribeca Film Center, and Merchant Ivory Productions. He is currently developing a sequel to *16 Acres*.

DARA McQUILLAN has worked or lived in Lower Manhattan since moving to New York from Ireland in 1996. He currently oversees the public relations, media, marketing, documentary, digital and communications aspects of the Silverstein organization's efforts to rebuild at the World Trade Center site. Dara began his career as a journalist at *Variety* in Los Angeles. He has also worked at Academy Award-winning Merchant Ivory Productions, Robert De Niro's Tribeca Film Center, and Universal Pictures. He studied at the University of Bologna, Italy, and at the University of St. Andrews, Scotland, where he graduated with a master's degree in philosophy.

INDEX

INDEX

A Century Downtown:

A Visual History of Lower Manhattan

Text © 2019 Matt Kapp

All images © their respective owners

and used with permission

Published in the United States by powerHouse Books,

a division of powerHouse Cultural Entertainment, Inc.

32 Adams Street, Brooklyn, NY 11201-1021

e-mail: info@powerHouseBooks.com

website: www.powerHouseBooks.com

First edition, 2019

Library of Congress Control Number: 2019947982

ISBN 978-1-57687-944-3

Book design by Chris Mueller

Printed by Pimlico Book International

10 9 8 7 6 5 4 3 2 1

Printed and bound in China